OPPORTUNITIES

in

DEC 0 3 2007

Architecture Careers

REVISED EDITION

ROBERT J. PIPER

WITHDRAWN

New York   Chicago   San Francisco   Lisbon   London   Madrid   Mexico City
Milan   New Delhi   San Juan   Seoul   Singapore   Sydney   Toronto

Library of Congress Cataloging-in-Publication Data

Piper, Robert J.
      Opportunities in architecture careers / by Robert J. Piper.—Rev. ed.
          p.   cm.
      Last ed. published 2001.
      ISBN 0-07-145868-9 (alk. paper)
        1. Architecture—Vocational guidance—United States.   I. Title.

  NA1995.P5   2005
  720.23'73—dc22   2005027003

  2 3 4 5 6 7 8 9 0   DOC/DOC   0 9 8 7

ISBN 0-07-145868-9

Interior design by Rattray Design

McGraw-Hill books are available at special quantity discounts to use as premiums and sales promotions, or for use in corporate training programs. For more information, please write to the Director of Special Sales, Professional Publishing, McGraw-Hill, Two Penn Plaza, New York, NY 10121-2298. Or contact your local bookstore.

This book is printed on acid-free paper.

Contents

FOREWORD

How do you find a school of architecture after dark? Look for the lights! While future doctors, lawyers, engineers, and scientists are studying in their dorms, the design studios in schools of architecture will often be filled throughout the night with students working to meet the deadline for their latest project. Those same students will take other courses in a traditional classroom setting, but the design studio is a unique part of their education as an architect. Here they are given their first challenge to create a solution to a specific problem. Here they begin to learn how to assemble the parts and pieces that make a building. Here they are often tired and feeling overwhelmed. But, if they are meant to be architects, they will sense that first stir of excitement that one day will peak when, as an architect, they see their ideas become reality.

Actually, learning to make a building is not easy. In fact, it is difficult. For a building to be considered architecture, it must protect those using it, serve its intended purpose, and be pleasing to the senses. To design such a building, an architect must spend years in the design studio and also be educated in the liberal arts and sciences. There are no easy courses in an accredited architecture curriculum. Math, physics, English, history, structural analysis, and other courses in construction methods and building materials are all part of an architectural curriculum.

When you earn your degree in architecture, you will have gained a quality education that will enable you to choose from a broad range of vocational opportunities. Many of those opportunities are identified in this book.

Before you decide you want to be an architect, consider your options carefully. Talk to an architect, listen to your high school counselor, try to get a summer job in an architect's office. If you do all of these things and are still interested in becoming an architect, be absolutely sure that you start on the right academic path. As a practicing architect—who also teaches architecture and serves as a regulator of the practice of architecture—I am sensitive to the plight of young men and women who, for lack of guidance, have strayed from that path. So here are the three essential steps that lead to your goal:

1. You must enroll in a school of architecture that is accredited by the National Architectural Accrediting Board (NAAB) and earn a professional degree in architecture. There are more than 140 such accredited programs to choose from. But be careful. You must have the NAAB-accredited degree. Some universities offer both accredited degrees and nonaccredited degrees and, unless you ask, they are not required to tell you which is which. So ask! Your future will be affected by the answer you get.

2. You must enroll in the Intern Development Program. Today almost every state either requires, or will soon require, that an archi-

tecture graduate enroll in and complete that program before he or she becomes eligible to take the Architect Registration Examination. The Intern Development Program is designed to help new graduates continue their education in architecture by gaining practical experience as preparation for taking the national exam.

3. After completing the Intern Development Program, you must take and pass the Architect Registration Examination. This is the last step required to become a registered architect in a single state.

To a young person, the steps on the path to becoming an architect may seem to be obstacles. But you will take them one step at a time, and if you want to reach your goal, you can.

How do I know? I'm not sure, but I'll tell you this. When our four children were growing up, my wife and I decided to build our own home. As an architect, I wanted my kids to be in a house that I had designed for them. Today those children are grown and have children of their own. Two of them are now members of our architecture firm—a fact that makes me proud as a father and as an architect.

Joseph P. Giattina Jr., FAIA
Past President
National Council of Architectural Registration Boards

1

CREATING THE
HUMAN ENVIRONMENT

THERE IS A body of knowledge that provides useful shelter for human activities and enduring inspiration for the human heart. Such knowledge is defined by the word *architecture*. Architects are the people who cause architecture, on purpose, as a business. Their special knowledge is also one of the prime ingredients that define architecture as a profession. The purpose of this book is to serve as a guide to a professional community where architects acquire and apply knowledge. Perhaps your reading and understanding of this book will eventually lead you to the practice of architecture.

At the outset of your lifelong study of architecture, make sure you include a visit to a construction site and spend time touring an architectural firm or two. Find an architect who will personally answer your questions. Most important, find a building that fills you with wonder. It is often in the experience of architecture where the will to build lives.

In the simplest terms, architecture is the art and science of designing buildings and the spaces between them. The spaces in and around buildings dictate how we move about and carry out our everyday activities, and, therefore, they are an extremely important part of our lives. Architecture is with us all the time—we live in it, play in it, work in it, and are seldom free from its influence.

Given this importance, a sense of quality must permeate the work of every architect. Certainly, we are all interested in quality in the work that we do. However, those who would practice architecture have a particular responsibility to produce quality work. After all, if architecture is one of the principal influences shaping human and community progress, a concern for quality architecture reflects the values of the community.

While those who choose architecture are choosing a career in creating the human environment, architects do not perform all the work required to create that environment; engineers, urban planners, landscape architects, construction contractors, brick masons, carpenters, financiers, building product manufacturers, and many others share in this endeavor. However, architecture is the basic art, the basic science, underlying the creation of the constructed environment. Thus, those trained in architecture will have many and varied career opportunities available to them.

You and Architecture

Look around you. Have you ever noticed the room in which you are now sitting? Its size and shape, the height of its ceiling, the distance between its walls and the placement of its doors and windows, the texture and patterns of its wall and floor materials, and how it fits in with other rooms in the building? Chances are the room is unique; you probably can't think of another one just like it.

It's like your friends—no two are alike. This uniqueness makes this room and the building of which it is a part a special place to you.

Now, if you look out the window and imagine yourself walking down the street passing your window, you realize the street and the buildings facing on it are different from all the others in your town. Yet, all together, these physical elements provide you with a room you know is yours, a house you feel is home, a school that is your own, a friendly neighborhood, a city of which you are proud, a country you love. These feelings result largely from your physical environment—the architectural surroundings in which you live, work, and play.

Now consider the details of your environment—the rug at your feet, the backyard bench, the street lamp at the corner. These, too, in all their varied sizes, colors, and textures, are part of your environment. They are the furnishings placed about in the architecture for your convenience and pleasure. They are the individual touches that mark these spaces as belonging to you alone or to your neighborhood alone. Architecture without such furnishings would be incomplete.

Then there are the vistas, sounds, smells, and weather that are part of your environment. In the countryside, architecture has nothing to do with creating these, but it can shape your experience of them to your advantage. Some, like a Nebraska sunset, a Gulf sea breeze, or a Michigan pine scent, you should be able to enjoy freely. Architecture should protect you from other natural elements, such as the bite of a Dakota winter or a humid Missouri summer. In the city, architecture has a great deal to do with creating as well as shaping parts of your environment.

Perhaps most important, your friends are also part of your environment—a very large part indeed. Architecture is nothing without people; when all is said and done, architecture and the physical environment that it creates are for people. This is something that should never be forgotten.

Need for Personnel

Once you recognize the importance of the environment to your own health, well-being, and awareness, it is hard to imagine that society can exist without the benefit of environmental designers. Unfortunately, building activity is a direct function of the health of the economy in general. When recessions occur, building slows down.

In the post–World War II period, from the late 1940s to the mid-1970s, there were not enough practitioners to fill existing positions within the design professions. With the economic recession of the mid-1970s, this situation changed. The schools that had attracted increasing numbers of students over the postwar years began to produce more graduates than the design professions could absorb. Consequently, many professionals left design practice and entered other fields to stay employed. Others expanded their practice activities to include development and construction of their own investment projects. This period introduced new career potentials to many individuals who found that their new careers were more suited to their talents. It also caused many of those who continued traditional private practice to step back and refine their design skills.

Still, it was a difficult time for recent graduates. Jobs were scarce. Many graduates found themselves returning to school for further education or traveling to broaden their perception and understanding of the art and science of architecture. Others simply took what they considered to be temporary jobs in other areas to wait for an opportunity to enter, full-time, into their chosen profession.

More recently, the recession of the early 1990s was followed by the building boom that is still with us today.

This cyclical pattern is always indicative of the nation's general economic health. To be sure, the nature of building activity will continue to change. There will eventually be less emphasis on new construction and greater emphasis on redevelopment, rehabilitation, and revitalization. More attention will be given to conservation, rather than exploitation, of our resources. More energy will be devoted to studying a problem and developing alternative solutions than to racing ahead with a solution that simply overwhelms the problem. These more reasoned approaches to problem solving will require greater and more refined talents than those required by our earlier, grosser techniques. It is also to be hoped that the design solutions reached will be more surely recommended and more rewarding to their developers.

Our society will definitely continue to seek well-trained and dedicated design talent. Graduates in architecture, engineering, landscape architecture, and urban planning should continue to find adequate career openings in their chosen professions. However, competition may be high for entry-level positions, especially in the most prestigious firms.

The actual demand for personnel within each profession will vary from year to year and from region to region. The vagaries of population growth, regional shifts due to climatic and resource pressure, individual mobility, and simple personal preferences as to lifestyle and environment play a very dynamic part in our nation's economic profile. You are a part of this profile, and where you choose to live and work contributes to the various statistics that you analyze in making that choice. Your choice, in turn, influences new federal, state, and local programs for urban revitalization, the creation of open space, the design and construction of transportation systems, the use and conservation of natural resources, and the development of countless programs in nations outside of our own country. All these activities add to the demand for design professionals.

Employment of architects is strongly tied to the level of local construction, particularly nonresidential structures such as office buildings, shopping centers, schools, and health care facilities, for example. Employment in nonresidential construction is expected to grow because the replacement and renovation of many industrial plants and buildings has been delayed for years and a large number of structures will have to be replaced or remodeled, particularly in urban areas where space for new buildings is becoming limited. On the other hand, technology enhancements will dampen demand for new commercial construction as nontraditional work and retail environments—such as teleconferencing, home offices, telecommuting, and electronic shopping—proliferate.

Because construction, particularly office and retail construction, is so sensitive to cyclical changes in the economy, architects will face especially strong competition for jobs or clients during recessions; consequently layoffs may ensue. Those involved in the design of institutional buildings, such as schools, hospitals, nursing homes, and correctional facilities, will be less affected by fluctuations in the economy.

There is little question that our colleges and universities can produce enough graduate design professionals to fill the demand. Some observers maintain that the schools are producing more graduates than the profession can absorb. Although this may be true of the design professions as narrowly defined in the historic sense, it is certainly not the case if the graduate views career opportunities in the broad sense advocated in this book. The employment outlook is always better for graduates who are flexible and who are openly willing to consider any opportunity to apply their talents, wherever that opportunity may arise.

Computers

What effect will the computer have on career opportunities in the design professions? Computers will increase rather than decrease total career opportunities in the design professions. Computerization of design functions—structural analysis, for instance—relieves the professional of the detail work formerly required in solving all sorts of design problems. It allows more time for the productive, creative work that no machine can do. To be sure, the computer has had a dramatic effect on the details of individual jobs; the drafter, for instance, has evolved into a specially trained computer graphics technician.

In the long run, the computer helps to increase productivity in what is a very labor-intensive field. For instance, today design professions and their construction associates are very concerned about land use, environmental impacts, resource allocation, and personnel policies. Addressing these concerns costs money, both in loss of productivity and in additional social cost. Although computerization cannot in itself relieve these pressures, it can assist the industry in comprehensively understanding and modeling them, and thus lower costs while increasing the industry's productivity. In fact, these results may prove to be the most beneficial of all consequences of computer usage.

Prospective architects who gain career-related experience in an architectural firm while they are still in school and who also know computer-aided design and drafting (CADD) technology, especially that which conforms to the new national standards, will have a distinct advantage in obtaining an intern position after graduation.

Age Limitations

There are no age limitations that are peculiar to the design professions as a discipline. Experience, as well as education, is a desirable characteristic of any endeavor. Most professionals do not reach peak earning or professional capacity until forty-five to fifty-five years of age. As for retirement, architects usually remain active for as many years as ability, stamina, and desire allow them to. It is also characteristic for the designer/architect to remain active in the community's social, cultural, political, and/or academic circles long after retirement from an active business career.

Diversity in the Profession

Until the 1970s, the status of women and minorities in both the environmental design professions and the construction industry was not very different than it was elsewhere in American business and industry. Generally speaking, opportunities for education in the professions were limited, and job openings were scarce. Once having secured employment, women found that their incomes were considerably lower than those of their male colleagues, and members of minorities found it difficult to advance.

Happily, this situation has been largely turned around. By the early 1970s, female and minority architects began to form organizations within the profession to examine the work environments and professional advancement opportunities that were available to them. In 1973 men and women members of the American Institute of Architects (AIA) brought their concerns to the attention of the general membership. This resulted in a study on the status of women and minorities in architecture. Existing employment practices were reviewed and subsequently acted upon to integrate women and minorities in all aspects of the profession as full participants. In 1974 a study committee within the AIA surveyed this situation and produced a landmark finding on the subject of women and ethnic minorities in the field of architecture. As a result, the AIA has been devoted to the development and promotion of long-range affirmative action programs for correcting any discrimination within the profession.

According to the most recent statistics released by the AIA, the roles of women and minorities in architecture have improved significantly over the last few years. A 2003 survey indicated that the previous two years had seen women and minorities achieve career advancement in architecture.

The last decade saw an increasing number of women and minorities enter the profession. In 2002 women comprised 27 percent of architecture staff at firms, up from 20 percent in 1999. Racial and ethnic minorities accounted for 17 percent, up from 9 percent three years prior. The figures for registered architects also reflect considerable progress. In 2002 women accounted for 20 percent of registered architects, up from under 14 percent in 1999, while racial and ethnic minorities were over 11 percent in 2002, up from 6 percent during the same period.

In addition, the rate at which women and racial and ethnic minorities have moved into leadership positions at firms has also increased. In 2002 women accounted for almost 21 percent of principals and partners at firms, up from 11 percent in 1999. Likewise, racial and ethnic minorities accounted for 11 percent of principals and partners in 2002, up from 5 percent in 1999.*

---

* American Institute of Architects. The Business of Architecture: The 2003 AIA Firm Survey Shows Significant Career Advances for Women and Minorities. www.aia.org/release_031110, accessed September 12, 2005.

Earnings

Income levels depend on several factors: company size, population densities, geography, local economies, and working patterns. Salaries for professionals will generally be higher in urban areas than in rural settings, but living expenses will also be higher.

Just as in other fields, earnings in the design professions are usually greater in private practice than they are in public employment, but public employment often provides the professional with greater opportunities to influence thinking in the field. This is especially true of urban and regional planning and of some fields of environmental planning. Obviously, income is only one employment consideration, and fringe benefits, cost of living, position, and job satisfaction must also be weighed to determine the attractiveness of a particular profession.

In 2005 median earnings for architects were $67,600. Principals in successful firms can earn well over $100,000. Earnings for other professionals involved in the building and design professions include urban and regional planners, $49,800; designers, $41,680; landscape architects, $47,400; and construction managers, $63,500.

In spite of all these factors, we can cite a few rules of thumb about the earning and work patterns of the design professions that have held true over the years:

- Earnings are generally higher in private practice than in public employment.
- There is a paid internship; the graduate makes a living wage immediately upon entering practice.
- Earnings fall into the median of all professionals, i.e., below doctors and dentists and about the same as lawyers and accountants.

- Incomes over $100,000 are becoming more and more common, especially in large firms.
- There is a great deal of geographic and job mobility because of personnel shortages.
- Construction is a cyclical industry, and incomes can vary according to local building activity.
- Deadlines are commonplace, often requiring overtime and evening work.
- Your clients must live with your work for a long time—both successes and failures.

Educational Requirements

Chapter 6 details the educational requirements for architecture, but we will take a moment here to comment on what is happening generally in education for the design professions.

In the past, architects, engineers, and landscape architects completed university training in four or five years. Advanced degrees have always been available, but the usual professional graduate entered practice after earning a bachelor of arts (B.A.) degree. Urban planners, on the other hand, have characteristically entered practice after earning a master of arts (M.A.) degree, based upon a B.A. in architecture, engineering, or a related discipline, plus the required graduate work of one to two years. In recent years, more and more students in all disciplines have been earning advanced degrees. In some cases, universities have dropped their undergraduate professional degrees and now expect students to go on to graduate work if they expect to become qualified professionals.

The design professions are upgrading their educational qualifications in response to the demand for more highly trained graduates. Should you consider an advanced degree? The answer is almost certainly yes if you seek to develop every skill and talent available to you in building your career. The advanced degree is becoming as common as the B.A. was previously. As always, those with the best qualifications will advance the most rapidly.

Licensing

Most professionals in the United States and Canada are licensed to practice their profession. The candidates must pass an examination given by the state or province of residence before they can practice medicine, law, architecture, or engineering. In most cases, these examinations are given some time after the individual has graduated, during which time he or she serves an internship in actual professional practice under the guidance of a licensed practitioner.

In the case of the design professions, the requirements for licensing vary. Architects and engineers are required to be licensed in every state, landscape architects in forty-six states. In any event, the chances are that if you choose to enter the design professions, you must plan on a period of internship followed by a licensing examination before qualifying as a professional.

The Vocation of Architecture

In broad terms, architects practice their vocation through understanding and coordinating all the resources for designing and building our physical environment. Architects in private practice render services directly to clients who compensate the architects for the time and expenses incurred in rendering the services.

In specific terms, architects can practice their vocation in the following ways:

- Maintaining an office of sufficient staff, size, equipment, and financing to render professional services
- Convincing potential clients that an architect should be retained to furnish the professional services that will be required by the client's proposed projects
- Entering into a written agreement with the client for the professional services required
- Preparing a written statement, called a *program*, describing in detail the requirements of the proposed project
- Executing agreements with consultants whose services may be required to supplement those of the architect
- Advising the client on the selection and suitability of sites for the proposed project
- Creating preliminary designs that satisfy the requirements of the program and the site
- Developing preliminary material selections, mechanical systems, cost analyses, construction time schedules, and financing alternatives for the proposed project
- Guiding the client to the selection of the single preliminary design that best solves the problems of program, site, cost, financing, and client wishes
- Coordinating the preparation of detailed drawings, specifications, and other contract documents required for construction of the project
- Detailing cost analyses and time schedules for the project's construction
- Assisting the client in the selection of various contractors required to complete the project and assisting in the execution of contracts between the client and the selected contractors

- Administering the construction contracts, including checking of drawings and other documents, materials, and workmanship furnished by the contractor; overseeing tests required on materials; certifying payments made to the contractor; and inspecting the project at completion
- Counseling the client on maintenance, repair, and remodeling requirements after completion of the project
- Managing daily business affairs, including answering correspondence, budgeting staff workloads, hiring and directing personnel, coordinating the work of consultants, interviewing salespeople, managing investments and personnel benefits, administering insurance programs, meeting payrolls and other current obligations, billing for services, promoting new projects, entertaining present and potential clients, and directing all office activities so that they respond to the legal and ethical requirements of the practice of architecture
- Responding to professional and civic responsibilities by overseeing the internship training of professional employees and participating in the programs of local civic and professional organizations

Nearly every project flowing through an architect's office will require most of the activities listed above. If the office has a staff of ten, chances are that it will have a minimum of six to eight major projects under way at any one time, in addition to several projects in either the "potential" or "nearly completed" stage, and a number of smaller projects involving only partial services. The aggregate of these office and business activities, plus those imposed upon the architect by reason of civic and professional obligations, gives you an idea of the wide range of aptitudes required of the architect.

2

ARCHITECTURE—PAST AND PRESENT

BEYOND YOUR PRESENT-DAY environment lie generations of work by architect-builders. The work of providing shelter began with the first people who piled stone upon stone, instinctively erecting a simple shelter for protection from enemies and the elements. That work, crude as it may seem today, was architecture; those early people were architects.

As people developed, their architectural horizons and technical abilities broadened, until today we are able to enclose entire cities in a single structure. With each historical period in this development, we can associate at least one particular form or style of architecture. These styles are always the result of three characteristics:

- **Natural characteristics.** Climate, altitude, geography, geology, and plant life determine what building materials are locally available and the requirements for weather protection in building construction.

15

- **Cultural characteristics.** Religious beliefs; patterns of trade, economy, and government; social ideals; and daily living habits determine the functions and activities to be accommodated in building design.
- **Technical characteristics.** There are three basic structural forms: post and beam, truss, and arch. These determine the means by which spaces are spanned, which in turn determine the open or column-free areas that can be contained within a building unit.

In knowing these characteristics, the architectural historian or archaeologist can identify a building with its place in the history of civilization. Thus, the significance of architectural styles is that they are a reflection of the period in which they evolved—of the people who lived at that time: their beliefs and aspirations, their environment, and their degree of cultural and technical achievement.

The Physical Embodiment of Human History

To fully appreciate the art and science of architecture, one should consider the role of architecture throughout history.

Early Architecture: Mesopotamia and Egypt

Architecture, as we think of it in terms of our Western culture, first appeared some six thousand years ago in Mesopotamia, a wedge of land between the Tigris and Euphrates Rivers in the country now called Iraq. The Babylonians and Assyrians who lived there believed in living for the moment and gave little thought to life after death. Consequently, their architecture was one of lush palaces and other lavish structures that reflected the everyday pleasures they valued. Mesopotamia was rich in clay, river water, and sunshine but provided little stone or timber, so sun-dried clay brick was a principal building material. Brick surfaces are easily molded into decorative forms, glazed with colored ceramic materials, or veneered with stone for decoration and weather protection. Consequently, major Babylonian buildings were covered with bas relief carvings, glazed friezes, or tooled stone veneers depicting incidents in the history of their civilization. Lacking quantities of stone or timber, these people were not able to span wide distances, and their buildings contained many columned spaces and small rooms. Had they known of the arch, they could have vaulted large spaces, even with brick. But the arch was not generally known or widely used until the early Romans first successfully employed it around 700 B.C.

Around 3000 B.C., the Egyptian civilization began in the Nile Valley. In contrast to those in Mesopotamia, the people of the valley believed that their everyday activities should be spent largely in preparation for life after death. Their tombs, in the form of pyramids and large rooms carved out of solid rock hillsides, were created to protect the deceased in their journey through eternal life.

Stone, a material of great crushing strength, is abundant in the Nile Valley. The Egyptians used it in quantity to construct post-and-beam buildings of great mass and height. These architectural forms were appropriate to the Egyptians' belief in the majesty and permanence of the afterlife. These bold forms combined with the brilliant sunshine to cause violent light and shadow patterns, which accentuated the massive design of the structures. The dry desert climate has preserved many Egyptian architectural masterpieces.

The Greek Empire

The Greek Empire in its Hellenic period (700–146 B.C.) brought the architectural foundation of our Western culture to full flower. The Greek form of government, academic and philosophical concepts, and cultivation of the arts combined to produce one of the world's great civilizations. Its architecture reflected this achievement; buildings were proportioned and detailed to a perfection of simplicity and harmony. Part of this success can be attributed to the availability of marble, a strong and beautiful building material that lends itself to exact detailing and fine surface treatment. These materials in the hands of artisans who valued the arts, freedom of mind and spirit, and personal achievement provided the ingredients for architectural excellence. The Greeks principally used a post-and-beam structural system, although they did introduce the truss for spanning large central building spaces. The gable roofs of many of their buildings reflected this structural element.

While the Greeks refined their aesthetics and used a "pure" geometry of circles, squares, and proportional systems, the Romans developed shapes based upon the demands of large-scale structures. They invented the advanced geometry of the ellipse, concrete, and the arch to produce monumental plazas bordered by heavily decorated buildings with huge vaulted interiors (500 B.C.–A.D. 500).

The Middle Ages and Renaissance

During the Middle Ages, superstitions and distrust caused people to withdraw behind the walls of heavily fortified cities or to crowd around the massive masonry walls of monasteries or the castle of a feudal lord (A.D. 400–1100). People depended on the monasteries or castles for protection; these structures were frequently sited on hilltops that provided sweeping views of the surrounding countryside and early warning of any approaching hostile force. Thick, high masonry walls topped with battlements reinforced the feeling of protection. Masons became extremely skillful, extending the use of stone even to roof construction, in which vaults employing the principle of the arch were used to span increasingly larger spaces. This time was known as the Romanesque Period. The spread of Christianity and the rebirth of scholarship are reflected in the period's development of the church plan based upon the Latin Cross, the ornamentation of doors and windows with carvings depicting religious figures, and the production of incredibly beautiful manuscripts describing the history and growth of the Christianity.

During the early 1200s, the fear and distrust of the Middle Ages began to give way to the need for greater communication and travel necessitated by increased commerce between cities. Feudal lords combined their resources, and the city-state emerged. People had became interested in the world around them and set out to explore what made humanity and nature work. This was the Renaissance Age. Its renewed interest in Greek and Roman cultural concepts, including classic architecture, reflected the classicism and humanism now associated with the period (A.D. 1200–1500).

During this time, builders became less interested in protection as an element of building design and construction and became more intrigued with pushing the performance of masonry to its limits. They emphasized height by using pointed arches and tall slender columns that soared from the floor to the peak of the building. They found they could punch great holes in the sidewalls by placing flying buttresses on the outside of the building to support the inner walls. They filled the openings with magnificent stained glass creations depicting events in human development. This period of Gothic architecture was the ideal reflection of the Western world's concurrent interest in expanding knowledge of and influence on nature and culture.

The Influence of Western Europe

The age of exploration and colonization spread Western European cultural characteristics throughout the world, and in our own hemisphere, we can note countless examples where these European influences combined with those of the American frontier to produce architectural styles unique to the New World (1300–1900).

During this same period, the powerful European monarchies competing for control of the New World rose to heights of unparalleled power in their own countries, and the architecture of such palaces as Windsor, Versailles, and El Escorial reflected their kingly stature. Political and social changes transformed most of these monarchies during the early years of the Industrial Revolution, shifting their power to varying forms of democratic government and their wealth to private industrial complexes (1700–present). The architecture of modern-day America is a reflection of the value our civilization places on private industry and democracy.

Thus, parallels between the characteristics of historical periods and the architecture they produced can be traced in every age of human development, including our own. As a final example, consider your high school or college building. It is probably a prominent structure in your community. It is built of materials readily available in your time and your area; it accommodates academic, athletic, and cultural activities that your community believes are important to your way of life; it incorporates contemporary structural techniques devised for enclosing the spaces required to house these activities. The architectural style of your school is a reflection of your time, your town, your beliefs, and your capabilities; its architect was a recorder of time, writing in the most appropriate materials available.

Architecture—Future Challenge

Your lifetime already includes interplanetary exploration and, perhaps, may include colonization. Here on Earth, undersea communities are foreseen. You can be sure that the styles of architecture developed during your lifetime will reflect these activities, for our nearly unlimited technical capacity to match dreams with reality is restricted only by the growing need for more intelligent conservation of our ever-scarcer environmental resources.

Conserving Resources

In thinking about the future, we should not undervalue the need for conservation of those resources. Concern for conservation will require increasing discipline from those who are responsible for advising society on the use of our limited resources. Fortunately, technological advancements—particularly in communications— make a much more refined use of our scarce resources possible. Moreover, improvements in communications and in the manipulation of basic data should give us earlier and more extensive information on the availability of scarce resources, therefore providing us with increasingly frequent cautions on the use of those resources.

If we regard this discipline as positive, we can see that our scientific development must take us toward the time when we will be able to synchronize our human needs with those of the other animals and occupants of our planet. We are preparing to build mini-environments in space and under the sea. These developments in the control of our climate and life resources will have vast effects upon our physical environment and the architecture accommodating that environment. The architects of your generation must respond to this challenge. If, in their response, they develop an architecture that is truly appropriate to its time, its place, and its function, they will have created an architecture as valid and important as was the Greek, Gothic, or any other historical style.

We best remember each past civilization at its moment of greatest achievement; that moment in history when the cultural elements of a civilization—its social, moral, ethical, political, and technical achievements—all seemed to be in balance. We also know that civilizations waned when these elements got out of balance. The architecture of a civilization is a reflection of this balance or imbalance.

Technical Advances

The years since the end of World War II have seen immense changes in the way we look at our physical environment and in the manner in which we attempt to manipulate it for our own enjoyment and convenience. From the late 1940s through the early 1960s, we sensed that there was scarcely any technical challenge that we could not overcome given the seemingly limitless technical expertise and natural resources available to us. Indeed, that remarkable period of innovation and growth produced a number of new building types intimately reflective of our feelings about the security of the present and the promise of the future. The interstate expressway system, the regional shopping center, the totally new suburban community, the international airport, the integrated petrochemical complex, the fantasy-land family recreation complex, the urban renewal project that completely rebuilt large chunks of our older cities, and the mixed-use urban developments are all examples of the remarkable vigor and energy so typical of those years.

The architecture of these projects reflected the time. Structural systems, mechanical systems, enclosure systems, graphics and signage systems, materials, and furnishings all became increasingly simplified and stripped down to their essentials in an effort to match productive capacities to the demands of a market that required buildings to accommodate increasingly large, complex functions. Mass production became an end in itself, and much of our physical environment seemed to take on a sameness or commonality: one housing area seemed to look like all the rest, few differences were apparent among the newer office buildings, each airport terminal was nearly indistinguishable from another. In the late 1960s and early 1970s, architecture's modern movement had reached a point where it seemed that its further refinement would produce little or no true advancement in the art and science of architecture.

A Cultural Shift

A modern movement had become institutionalized as a direct reflection of what had happened to our society in general. In the late 1960s and early 1970s, society reacted, sometimes violently, seeking to change our institutions by giving greater recognition to the value of diversity and worth of the individual. Concurrently, we discovered that our resources were limited and that money and technology alone could not solve all our contemporary problems. The conservation movement, the equal rights movement, the citizen participation movement, and a host of other societal concerns regarding criminal justice, health planning, the elderly, the handicapped, and community and family history all are products of this fervor. These phenomena have had their effect on architecture.

One of the most notable effects has been the growth in the rehabilitation and restoration of existing structures. The tremendous growth in our economy following World War II promoted an almost universal attitude that new was better than old, and a basic assumption that growth could only be accommodated in new, fresh structures placed upon previously undeveloped land. "Technological obsolescence" in building materials and systems was seen as the prime criteria for abandoning or demolishing the old and replacing it with the latest and most advanced material or device developed by our technological capacities. The thirst for newness became a cult, a throwaway economy replaced a concern for tradition and respect for heritage; individualism was replaced by the "man in the grey flannel suit." But society is resilient. And in the later 1970s and early 1980s, individualism returned, bringing with it nostalgia for the old, increased perception of historical values, and an appreciation of the contribution of the individual.

In the 1980s a sophisticated experimentation with classical symbols and decoration was known popularly as *Postmodernism*. It was a period of unusual freedom of choice for the architect. Certainly, a principal goal of the Postmodernist movement was to join with society in general in the search for institutions that provided a better balance between technology, resources, and the rights and responsibilities of the individual. Part of the increased formal variety was made possible by computer technology in the design process and in industry. Our global economy also has increased access to products and craftsmanship. The Internet has transformed communication as well as the business world.

Toward the Future

Since the beginning of the Industrial Revolution, technical achievements have tended to develop more rapidly than other cultural concepts; society has constantly sought a better balance between technology and popular culture. Now that society is demanding a better balance and our computerized work world promises us more time to devote to social, moral, ethical, and political pursuits, we may be approaching the time when achievements in nontechnical concepts will match technical achievements. If so, the level of architectural taste demanded by our contemporary culture will be at once gratifying and challenging to the architectural profession. The promise of such balance is closer to achievement than it has been for generations. Your generation may see it accomplished.

3

THE PROFESSIONAL ARCHITECT

BY READING THIS book, you are preparing yourself to choose a vocation. A vocation is a regular occupation or profession; specifically, one for which you are especially suited or qualified.

When you choose a particular kind of work, you are selecting a part of the business world that you find attractive and believe would offer the best opportunity for the gainful employment of your unique talents. You are choosing an occupation. For some people, this first choice is sufficient and they follow their chosen occupation for forty to fifty productive years, developing their talents to a fine degree and marketing them for satisfying monetary rewards. Indeed, the standard of living you presently enjoy is largely the result of just such an application of talents.

For many other people, an occupation alone is not sufficient; they want to do more than simply work at a chosen occupation. Some people believe that in carrying out everyday work activities, service to others becomes more important than personal recognition or the accumulation of wealth. You will find persons with this outlook in all walks of life: for instance, the farmers who tend the soil so they leave it more productive than they found it; the administrator who insists on excellence in working conditions as well as worker performance; the businessperson who not only markets a quality product but also backs its performance with a personal guarantee of service. Such people have deep personal commitments to the well-being of humanity and believe strongly in their personal responsibility to serve this commitment.

This kind of personal outlook is a basic attitude required of those who enter theology, law, medicine, architecture, engineering, education, urban planning, and other disciplines devoted to the service of humanity. Such disciplines are called the professions. Their hallmark is basic concern for people—their health, safety, and general welfare. This ideal is popularly referred to as "protection of the public interest." An appreciation of the obligations and responsibilities that accompany this concern is essential to entering a profession. This chapter examines these obligations and responsibilities because this commitment to the public interest will require that you dedicate yourself to intensive study and practice throughout your formal education and your professional career.

The Public Interest

All of us have a commitment to the protection of the public interest. That is, each of us as a citizen has a responsibility to uphold the law, to support our public institutions, and to conduct our personal affairs in a manner that does not injure our fellow citizens. As members of society, we develop rules of conduct, procedures for settling disputes, and methods for the organization of our government. Collectively, these systems serve to protect our health, safety, and general welfare.

The professional's responsibility is not only to promote the observance of these laws and procedures as a citizen, but to apply them in daily practice, interpret their intent for other citizens, defend their application where required, and suggest their modification by society when and where it seems appropriate. To exercise this responsibility properly, professionals must have an overriding interest in the welfare of others. For the doctor, this interest exhibits itself in a concern for the health and physical well-being of the community; for the lawyer, in a concern for law and justice equally applicable and available to all; for the architect, in a concern for a functional, safe, and pleasing physical environment.

But the professional does not act alone in discharging these responsibilities. The professional depends upon others—clients—to present problems that require the exercise of the professional's judgment based on previous training and experience. This is how the professional earns a fee. Characteristically, then, the professional stands somewhere between the client's interest and the public interest and has a responsibility to find a way that both are served. This is not an easy task. It often requires that the professional frankly advise the client that the problem can't be solved without violating the public interest. Just as often, it will require that the professional vigorously defend the client's position and advocate a modification of a popularly held attitude or belief, or a change in the application of a public rule or regulation. Frequently, then, the professional will advise a client to take a certain action based upon moral and technical issues that may have little or nothing to do with the amount of the fee, the client's profit, or any other monetary issues involved.

Requirements of the Profession

To prepare for such a career, you will be required to undertake formal schooling ranging from five to seven years in an accredited professional school, serve an apprenticeship after graduation, and pass an examination for licensure administered by your state of residence. Upon entering practice, you will be expected to uphold and defend both the rules and regulations established by the public to govern the practice of your profession and certain other codes of ethics or standards of practice developed by your peers to guide you in the exercise of your professional responsibilities.

Maintaining these rules and regulations will remain your responsibility throughout your professional career. Furthermore, the technical advancements and refinements in your field of interest after you graduate will undoubtedly require that you periodically return to the classroom for refresher courses in certain techniques or to learn new technologies. Indeed, depending on your special interests, you may return to school many times over several years of practice and thereby earn an advanced degree or two in highly specialized fields.

The demands that are made upon students and practitioners of any profession should not be minimized. The periods of study, internship, and licensure noted above are intensive, and similar burdens continue throughout the professional's career. And not to be forgotten, professional study is comparatively expensive, and the beginning income of many professionals is often below that of the average college graduate.

There are rewards, of course, and they are intrinsic as well as material: the satisfaction of exercising personal independent judgment in solving another's problems; the joy of creating and successfully executing such solutions; the appreciation of clients and a public satisfactorily served; the recognition that results from professional success.

Knowing these demands and rewards, you should consider the following questions at this point in your search for a career:

- **Personal character.** Can you meet the high standards of character and conduct required of one who acts as a professional adviser?
- **Human understanding.** Do you have the patience and understanding to deal with people as their professional adviser?
- **Stamina and discipline.** Do you have the stamina to see yourself through years of intensive study, and the sense of personal discipline to shape your professional growth throughout your career?
- **Rewards.** Are you willing to accept the intrinsic rather than material rewards characteristically associated with having a professional career?

If you can answer yes to each of these points, you have the basic attitudes required for the rigors of a professional career.

The Profession of Architecture

Architecture is for people, and the foremost purpose of any building is to provide functional, healthful, safe, and pleasing shelter for human activity. A building affects not only its occupants, but also its period of history and all those who come into contact with it. If a building is to be successful, its design must be appropriate to its time in history, to its place in the community, and to its function as a shelter. Its construction must be economical, safe, and of sound, well-maintained materials. The architectural profession must advise the public and the construction industry in the production of buildings that answer these criteria, and the individual architect must design these buildings and administrate the contracts for their construction. By discharging these responsibilities in their day-to-day practices, the members of the architectural profession protect the public interest while creating our constructed physical environment.

Any profession so vitally concerned with the protection of the public interest will develop certain private organizations and public regulative devices to help it advance the art and science of its profession. Thus architecture—like other recognized professions such as law, medicine, dentistry, and accounting—exhibits four organizational and regulative devices characteristic of such professions.

First, there is a defined field of knowledge. As previously noted, the art and science of architecture date from the efforts of the first people who piled stone on stone to create shelter for protection from the elements. In the intervening centuries, architectural knowledge has become a well-defined and developed field of human activity.

Second, there is an accredited system of education to prepare professionals for practice. Today there are 113 colleges and universities in the United States offering courses leading to degrees in architecture; there are 10 such schools in Canada. Each of these schools is fully accredited by public and private agencies appointed to periodically review their course content and to issue accreditation credentials.

Third, there is a required period of postgraduate internship followed by a publicly administered examination leading to licensure to practice. Each of the fifty states as well as the District of Columbia, Guam, Puerto Rico, and the Virgin Islands have laws requiring internship and examination prior to licensure to practice architecture. Canadian provinces impose comparable standards. Internship and licensing periods in the architectural profession are more fully discussed later in the book.

Fourth, there is a recognized practicing profession dedicated to the promotion of the public interest through the advancement of its science, art, education, internship, and standards of practice. In 1857 a group of practicing architects formed The American Institute of Architects for these very purposes. Today, a majority of architects of professional status in the United States are members of the AIA and its more than three hundred chapter and state associations. More than sixty other nations from Argentina to Yugoslavia have organizations similar to the AIA serving the public and the architectural professions in their own countries. In Canada, the Royal Architecture Institute of Canada (RAIC) is the association that oversees the practice of architecture.

The AIA Code of Ethics

The American Institute of Architects renders dozens of services to the public and to its members on matters of architectural and urban design, education, research, office practice, building materials and services, legislation, and public relations. Its foremost function, however, is to maintain the ethical and professional standards of the profession. These are embodied in its Code of Ethics and Professional Conduct, 2004 edition. Excerpts from that document will illustrate the high standards of ethical and professional performance the members of AIA demand of themselves.

The Code is based upon the age-old realization that the profession of architecture calls for practitioners of integrity, culture, acumen, creative ability, and skill. The services of an architect may include those appropriate to the development of our physical environment, provided that the practitioner's professional integrity is maintained and that the services rendered further the ultimate goal of creating an orderly and beautiful environment. Further, it is recognized that the architect, as a professional, should seek opportunities to advance the health, safety, beauty, and well-being of the community. In other words, the architect has moral obligations to society beyond the requirements of law or business practices. In fulfilling the client's needs, the architect must always consider the public good and interest.

The Code also speaks to the architects' ethical and professional conduct in three ways:

1. By specifying broad principles of conduct
2. By spelling out ethical standards that are more specific than the usual broad principles of conduct and that are both goals toward which members of the AIA should aspire and guidelines for their professional performance and behavior
3. By specifying rules of conduct that are mandatory, their violation being subject to disciplinary action by the AIA

In their totality, the specifications of the Code lay out a rounded set of operating guidelines for the professional conduct of members in the pursuit of their professional activities wherever they may occur.

It will be sufficient for our purposes here to note examples of the various kinds of statements mentioned above, the broad principles of conduct, the more specific ethical standards, and the rules of conduct.

The five canons or broad principles of conduct of the Code are as follows:*

Canon I: General Obligations. Members should maintain and advance their knowledge of the art and science of architecture, respect the body of architectural accomplishment, contribute to its growth, thoughtfully consider the social and environmental impact of their professional activities, and exercise learned and uncompromised professional judgment.

Canon II: Obligations to the Public. Members should embrace the spirit and letter of the law governing their professional affairs and should promote and serve the public interest in their personal and professional activities.

Canon III: Obligations to the Client. Members should serve their clients competently and in a professional manner, and should exercise unprejudiced and unbiased judgment when performing all professional services.

Canon IV: Obligations to the Profession. Members should uphold the integrity and dignity of the profession.

Canon V: Obligations to Colleagues. Members should respect the rights and acknowledge the professional aspirations and contributions of their colleagues.

The Ethical Standards (abbreviated E.S.) are articulated in the Code with respect to each canon. For example, the Ethical Standards listed under Canon V shown above are as follows:

---

* Provisions from the Code of Ethics and Professional Conduct are reproduced with permission from the American Institute of Architects. The 2004 version of the Code is available at www.aia.org/about_ethics.

E.S. 5.1 Professional Environment. Members should provide their associates and employees with a suitable working environment, compensate them fairly, and facilitate their professional development.

E.S. 5.3 Professional Recognition. Members should build their professional reputation on the merits of their own service and performance and should recognize and give credit to others for the professional work they have performed.

The Rules of the Ethics Code are mandatory actions pertaining to each Ethical Standard. A rule that applies to E.S. 5.3 above is Rule 5.302:

Members leaving a firm shall not, without the permission of their employer or partner, take designs, drawings, data, reports, notes, or other materials relating to the firm's work, whether or not performed by the Member.

The force and validity of the AIA Code of Ethics and Professional Conduct is such that it serves as a measure of the practitioner's dedication to the architectural profession. It is not necessary to become a member of the AIA if you become registered, but similar standards of practice have frequently been cited by several states' licensing and registration agencies in their examination of candidates for licensure and enforcement of registration requirements.

Attitudes and Aptitudes

Earlier in this chapter we discussed the personal attitudes required of those considering a professional career and suggested that you candidly examine yourself in light of these requirements. Briefly, these attitudes were the following:

- Personal character
- Capacity for human understanding
- Physical stamina and self-discipline
- Satisfaction with intrinsic rather than material rewards

To these we add the aptitudes required of those considering a career in architecture. You should candidly examine your own talents in light of these requirements. They are described below:

- **Imagination.** Are you a creative dreamer, an ideas person? Do you usually have several suggestions on how to deal with a situation or solve a problem? Architectural practice requires the continuous production of new and creative solutions to design and construction problems.
- **Common sense.** Do you have a faculty for sound judgment? Can you balance the ideal and desirable with the practical and achievable? Architectural solutions must be practical as well as stimulating if they are to result in construction.
- **Enthusiasm.** Are you a person of keen and ardent interests? An architect must be able to project ideas and philosophies to others. The architect's ideas are of little value if they cannot be sold to others.
- **Diplomacy.** Can you work with others? Can you accept their ideas and thoughts and merge them with your own? Building design and construction involves hundreds of people, all of whom look to the architect for general direction and guidance.

- **Visualization.** Can you visualize space, color, and texture? The very essence of architecture is delight—the pleasant stimulation of the senses. The architect determines the potential delight of a space as it is designed.
- **Propriety.** Do you have a sense of what is appropriate, timely, and suitable? Successful architecture is always appropriate to its time, place, and function.
- **Synthesis.** Can you cope with a variety of details and meld them into a coherent, rational whole? A building design incorporates tremendous amounts of detailed information.
- **Perseverance.** Can you see a project through to its completion in spite of delays and pressures? The usual building project is stretched out over many months of work and typically encounters periods of delay while awaiting decisions and periods of overtime work to meet deadlines.
- **Technology.** Do you have a faculty for mathematics, engineering, and other scientific and technical concerns? Contemporary building design and construction is as much a science as an art. The architect deals daily with structural, mechanical, sanitary, illuminative, power, and other technological problems.
- **Massing.** Can you judge the distances between things and their bulk, height, length, and width? Architecture involves size and shape, and the architect must have a good eye for the size of things.
- **Communication.** Can you express your ideas graphically, orally, and in writing? Obviously, the architect must be able to draw—both freehand as well as mechanically, using a variety of drafting instruments and aids. These require a refined sense of color, economy of line, and the use of shade

and shadow. But the practice of architecture involves an immense amount of writing also, much of it quite technical. There are also countless occasions where the architect must rely on verbal imagery to explain ideas to others.

- **Management.** Do you have a sense of business and personnel administration? The architect brings together many people and interests to produce a building and manages the expenditure of considerable sums of money in doing so.

If you can answer yes to each of these points, you have the basic aptitudes required for the rigors of a career in architecture.

The architects in your hometown can be a great help in determining whether this profession is the right match for your aptitudes and attitudes. Do not hesitate to contact the local chapter of The American Institute of Architects to request the names and addresses of one or more practitioners whom you might call upon to discuss your choice of career. Visit www.aia.org and select "architect finder" to look for your local AIA chapter and the names of architects practicing in your area. Once you have selected an architect, call and explain your mission and ask for an appointment for an office interview. Be on time, have your questions firmly in mind, and record important points for later reference. You will find the experience immensely rewarding, and the practitioner will be pleased to have had an opportunity to assist you in the choice of a career.

In preparing for such an interview, you should review the questions you expect to ask with your vocational counselor. Chances are that you have already talked with the counselor about your search for a vocation and found the discussion to be helpful in thinking out solutions to the many questions that have come to mind. By discussing your interview with the counselor before and after your visit to the architect's office, you will get the maximum benefit from your interview.

If by chance you haven't yet called upon your school's vocational counselor, or would like to know more about career planning before you do have your meeting, it is recommended that you check references in your school's library under "Vocational Guidance." There should be several available that will provide you with a general background on choosing a vocation.

To Be an Architect

This concludes our discussion of the responsibilities, obligations, and rewards of the professional architect, as well as the profession and vocation of architecture. Later chapters detail the educational, internship, and licensing requirements you must meet if you are someday to enter such practice.

By now you recognize that if you choose a career in architecture, you also choose to devote your adult life to searching out, understanding, and coordinating all the resources required for building our physical environment, and in so doing, protecting the public interest in the design and construction of buildings and the spaces between. As we have noted, the demands placed upon professional architects are great, but so are the rewards. Architecture can be seen, felt, lived in, and used; architecture shapes our lives, adds beauty to our world, and, if fine enough, its influence will last long after its creator is gone. Most important is the fact that, if you choose to be an architect, you know that your work will make a contribution to the present and future welfare of your community.

4

The Construction Industry

As already mentioned, construction is a cyclical industry, meaning it reflects fluctuations in the national economy sensitively and rapidly. During economic recessions construction is often put off, whereas in times of economic growth, the industry may find it difficult to keep up with the demand for its product. Since construction is so important to our economy, all levels of government have developed policies on the construction of public works in an attempt to minimize economic fluctuations. Extensive public construction projects are often undertaken in times of recession to stimulate a lagging economy.

Many other elements of the American economy join with the construction industry in building and maintaining our physical environment. Your school, for instance, contains thousands of separate products supplied by many different sources. Each product was conceived, designed, manufactured, shipped, and assembled through the employment of labor, materials, and capital supplied by various elements of our economy. To these activities must be added those required for daily servicing, maintaining, and repairing your school if we are to identify all those elements of our national economy that participate in the creation and maintenance of this single piece of your physical environment.

The many vocations included in the construction element of our national economy can be grouped into three general classifications:

- **The design group.** Architects, engineers, and other professionals and technicians who design our physical environment
- **The constructor group.** Contractors, suppliers, manufacturers, and workers in other building trades who construct our physical environment
- **The support group.** Financiers, realtors, educators, insurance underwriters, testers and researchers, public administrators, and others who supply land, loan money, train personnel, and perform other services ancillary to the creation of our physical environment

While a common thread of interest—that of construction—runs through all three groups and touches each person involved, there are considerable differences in individual motivations that lead each person to a particular type of work within the industry.

The Design Group

The design group includes people who have a basic interest in conceiving, programming, synthesizing, and planning our physical environment. These are people who think "in the round," and can visualize the effects of various relationships in space, color, texture, warmth, and light without first having to see, feel, or otherwise experience them. Characteristically, these are highly skilled and trained people with refined senses for what is appropriate to particular types of environments and functions. Typically, people in this group regard themselves as professionals who place service to society and their profession above any personal gain.

The Constructor Group

Those in the constructor group are people of action. They want to experience the construction process firsthand, to work directly with the machines and materials used in the building process, and to see the building rise as a direct result of their efforts. Many of them are businesspeople—contractors, suppliers, manufacturers—who, by the astute management of personnel and machines, earn substantial monetary rewards in their various vocations.

The Support Group

The motivations and interests of those in the support group are as varied as the list of professions would indicate. The trades in this group render many vital services to the construction industry and, in turn, look to construction for a large share of their daily endeavors. Frequently, they must be as knowledgeable of the workings of the construction industry as the designers and constructors, and may well have gained their education or started their careers in those fields.

This summary of construction industry prospects and of the vocations encompassed within the industry gives you an idea of the breadth and potential of career opportunities it offers. You should particularly note that those who choose a career in design are at the heart of the industry; their decisions put other elements of the industry into action. Consequently, those trained in architecture find their careers can carry them in many directions throughout the industry—into engineering, construction, finance, manufacturing, public administration—as well as into design.

Constructing a High School

To illustrate the broad potential of those trained and experienced in architecture, let us consider the design and construction of a high school.

Planning

To start the process, the board of education and the superintendent of schools determine that a new school building is required. Their decision is based on the need for more space to accommodate a growing student population, or perhaps an existing school needs replacement. In either case, architectural services are required to help them decide where to locate the school, what facilities to include, and the approximate cost. An architect in private practice is retained to conduct studies on location, function, and cost and to assist the school board and the administration in making their decision.

The private practice of architecture engages by far the greatest number of architects in the United States. It offers the opportunity to own and operate your own business and professional enterprise and to share in all the challenges and rewards of being your own boss and directing your own affairs.

Public agencies, such as your school district, often employ architects on their administrative staffs who perform in-house architectural services on buildings that house agency functions. They also work with architects in private practice when the agency undertakes major building projects. Such public agency positions offer rewarding careers to those architects attracted to public service.

In making studies on location, the architect working for the school district consults with local city planning commissions on plans for neighborhood development. In this stage of the process, architects contribute to urban design as members of the planning commission, employees of the commissioner's staff, or private planning consultants. Urban planning is a challenging field for those trained in architecture. Architects with special interests in urban design, geography, sociology, economics, or public administration have many career opportunities either as private consultants or as staff members of federal, state, and local agencies concerned with urban development.

As the architect and the school board study the functions and activities to be included in your school building, they call in special consultants on various educational planning problems, such as television and team teaching, visual aids, and auditorium and stage design. Some architects in private practice specialize in particular kinds of buildings: for instance, schools, theaters, hospitals, or shopping centers. Others specialize in particular functions within a building, such as kitchen and cafeteria areas, hospital operating suites, or X-ray and radiology rooms. As a building-type consultant, an architect has an opportunity to concentrate on those areas of the construction industry he or she finds of greatest interest.

To develop cost figures for constructing and maintaining the school building through the issuance of bonds, the school board and the architect consult with taxing and bonding authorities expert in the field of construction financing. Construction requires loan money; that is, money loaned to the owner of the building—in this case your school board—by commercial institutions, such as banks and insurance companies whose business it is to supply money. Such lending institutions offer unusual career opportunities for architects with particular interests in construction economics and finance. Further, many such institutions deal principally with public construction that is financed through tax and bond revenues. These institutions offer additional career openings for architects knowledgeable in public finance and tax administration.

Having determined that the school should be built, the school board directs the architect to prepare detailed drawings and specifications for the construction of the building. The architect then brings together and directs a team of professionals and technicians skilled in the many disciplines required in building design and construction. Most of these talents are members of the architect's staff. For certain specialized areas of design, the architect retains other private consultants to assist in the preparation of the drawings and specifications. The design of contemporary buildings requires architectural designers, structural engineers, mechanical engineers, specification writers, interior designers, planners for special equipment, draftsmen, and a whole host of special supporting talents such as computer programmers, statisticians, technical writers, systems analysts, researchers, business administrators, and estimators. Those trained in architecture can specialize in any of these fields, depending upon their desires, talents, and special education.

Members of the design team call in a number of materials and building systems experts—often representatives or salespeople from various building product manufacturers—requesting information and recommendations on the use and limitations of hundreds of different products considered during the design process. The sophisticated technology of present-day building materials requires manufacturers' representatives to be educated and trained in technology and research as well as in sales. Architects whose special talents lie in product design and development, or in sales, will find many career opportunities with manufacturers.

As the drawings and specifications are developed, the architect checks with federal, state, and local public agencies to determine that the building design conforms to code. Public agencies responsible for the administration of building codes and other regulations affecting construction offer rewarding careers for architects interested in public health and safety.

As the detailed drawings and specifications are completed, they are combined with insurance and legal documents developed by attorneys and insurance underwriters retained by the school board. The legal, insurance, and bonding elements of the construction industry afford many career openings for those who are trained in architecture and who also have an interest in finance or law.

Once the drawings, specifications, and related construction contract documents are completed, building contractors are invited to review them, estimate the cost of the labor and materials involved, and then submit a bid for constructing the school. This bidding process takes about thirty days, during which time each contractor calls upon many other people to help complete the estimates.

Suppliers are asked to estimate the cost of furnishing and delivering concrete, brick, pipe, wire, and many other materials that the contractor's own workers will put together at the site. Manufacturers are contacted to estimate the cost of those parts of the building that are to be factory-fabricated and shipped to the school site ready for installation. Subcontractors estimate the cost of those portions of the construction work that the contractor expects to assign to them, such as drywall, ceiling tile, and painting.

The contractor goes through every detail in the documents, mentally constructing the building; determining the construction technique required; planning the use of equipment; checking each estimate received from suppliers, manufacturers, and subcontractors; and coordinating and scheduling all phases of the work so that the school will be completed efficiently, expeditiously, and economically. Construction management—the scheduling of construction work, estimating and controlling its cost, and coordinating its many separate operations—is of vital importance to the construction industry. Historically, construction managers have risen within the ranks of the constructors. With the increasing complexity of building design and the advent of computerized scheduling and costing techniques, there is an ever-growing demand in construction management for architects and engineers having that unique combination of talents—design plus management plus administration skills.

Construction

When the contractors complete their estimates, each submits a bid to the school board and the architect. A construction contract is signed between the board and the contractor submitting the lowest dollar bid, and the construction begins.

Construction of your school will probably take from ten to eighteen months, depending on the size of the project. During construction, countless decisions are made regarding construction methods, materials, and techniques required to produce the result called for in the contract documents. The architect and consultants participate in this process by providing important interpretations and clarifications of the documents as they were requested by the contractor. Just as important are the interpretations of the architect's intent that are rendered by the contractor and by hundreds of other persons responsible for producing the parts of the finished school. Subcontractors, manufacturers and suppliers, testing and inspecting agencies, insurance and bonding agents, financing sources, and the school board itself participate in this ongoing decision-making process.

Building construction provides many rewarding opportunities for the construction technician whose special expertise in construction superintendence, drafting, testing and inspection, factory production of component parts, or similar services contribute to the construction of a building through the interpretation of architectural drawings and specifications.

As construction progresses, the public improvements required to service the school—including roads, sanitary and storm drainage, water and utility lines—are constructed by appropriate public agencies. Although such improvements are not actually a part of the building project, they are made necessary by it, and their design and construction must be coordinated with that of the school. The design and construction of public improvements by federal, state, and local agencies, and by private utilities offer rewarding career opportunities for architects who wish to devote their talents to a public service career.

The Finishing Touches

Site improvements and landscaping are undertaken next. Athletic fields and courts, playground equipment, access roads and parking lots, walks, fencing, lighting, sod, and plantings are placed, and the school begins to look like a permanent part of the community. Landscape design, site planning, and construction demand a unique kind of architectural talent—a combination of building design, landscape architecture, civil engineering, and urban design.

Interior finish, furnishings, and equipment are completed next. Furniture, rugs, draperies, library shelving, cafeteria equipment, auditorium seating, stage lighting and curtains, science tables, gymnasium equipment, and hundreds of other finish and equipment items are installed. Interior design, including design of special service equipment, graphics, and signage, offers interesting and varied careers to architects who wish to focus their talents on creating harmonious, stimulating, and serviceable interior environments.

The school is complete. As a significant statement of its time and place, it is of interest to other people and other communities. Press releases are sent to local and national news media representatives, some of whom visit the completed school to gather additional information for dissemination through radio, television, magazines, and newspapers.

Architectural journalism and architectural photography, including architectural criticism and real estate commentary, are inviting fields for those trained in architecture who have complementary talents in writing or photography. In this age of communication and interpretation, such talents are in great demand.

Maintenance

Following the school's completion, continuing maintenance and repair, and perhaps remodeling, will be needed to adapt the school to changing educational demands. Such postcompletion programs, if not responsive to the building design's original intent, can drastically restrict its successful operation. Professional services in building maintenance, repair, and remodeling afford unusual opportunities to architects who seek a career combining design with performance evaluation testing, research, and development.

The cycle of activities begun by the decision to build a new school is completed years later when the school board makes arrangements for the abandonment and sale of the existing school facilities. They announce the intended sale of the building and call for purchase bids from interested developers. Chances are that the school has become a community landmark. People interested in its preservation as a landmark speak out and ask that the building not be demolished, that it be somehow retained as essential to the historical record of the community's culture and growth.

Historic preservation is a field of growing interest to architects and one that promises increased opportunities for career pursuit. The historic preservationist must have a comprehensive knowledge of historic architectural styles and the contribution of these styles to a given community's artistic and historic environment. As important, however, is the ability of the historic preservationist to suggest and document adaptive uses that might be made of valued buildings that have outlived their original functional purpose. This requires a talent for putting together packages of uses and ownership arrangements that make it economically feasible to retain the building for some other use while retaining the integrity of those features of the building that make it a landmark. Finally, the preservationist must be intimately knowledgeable of craftsmanship and construction techniques required for authentic rehabilitation of older buildings.

This brief discussion of the design, construction, and maintenance of a school and the recycling of its older facilities is a practical illustration of the broad range of career opportunities offered by the construction industry and open to those with basic training and experience in architecture. You can see that architecture, while basically a matter of environmental design, prepares students for entrance into countless other disciplines. Indeed, this broad career potential is a prime advantage to those trained and experienced in architecture.

5

THE ARCHITECT'S PRACTICE

WHILE CAREER MOBILITY has always been a unique feature of the American economy, contemporary cultural mores have made it even easier for people to change career orientations during their working years. This is particularly true of the white-collar worker or the professional. In the professions, one increasingly finds doctors, lawyers, engineers, and other highly trained individuals working outside of their profession, as that profession is strictly defined. A person with several talents and motivations may be better equipped to cope with rapid changes in technology and resultant fluctuations in employment opportunities.

As noted throughout this book, the environmental design and construction industry has its fair share of advances and changes in the technology and economics of the industry, with the consequent ups and downs of employment opportunities. Within the industry, however, those trained and experienced in architecture have qualifications that will allow them to move into a number of disciplines embraced by the design professions and construction industry.

In the 1960s, approximately 90 percent of the licensed architects in the United States were engaged in private architectural practice. In the late 1990s, that percentage dropped to the mid-80th percentile, with architects migrating to other interest areas such as government, industry, educational institutions, and research. These figures indicate significant shifts from private architectural practice into related design disciplines such as urban planning and into other work environments—for instance, public policy agencies, development, research, writing, teaching, and industry.

In 2002, one in five architects was self-employed, which is about three times the proportion for all professional and related occupations. In this chapter we will examine the details of private architectural practice—what it is today and what it is likely to be when you enter practice some six to eight years from now.

The Scope of Architectural Practice

The private practice of architecture is a business in every sense of the word, and the practicing architect is a businessperson as well as a professional. The architect's primary motivation for entering practice is a professional desire to practice the art and science of architecture. However, the practitioner also expects to manage a practice profitably and ethically, thereby gaining a place in local public affairs as a successful businessperson and respected citizen. This requires constant attention to the scope of the practice, that is, to a number of general concerns affecting the content of practice and the conditions under which the profession is pursued.

Content of Practice

The first and most dominant concern is for the nature and quality of services the architect provides the client. The details of these architectural services will be discussed later in this chapter. However, note that the primary objective of the architect's services has always been, and must always remain, the union of function (the planning and relationships of spaces that meet human needs) with structure (the method of enclosing or defining space) and with beauty (that quality without which no space can qualify as architecture). This unity is what we call *design*; it is the very essence of architectural services.

Second, the architect in private practice is concerned with the professional responsibilities discussed in Chapter 3. The prime focus is the responsibility to protect the public interest through the design of buildings and the spaces between them.

The architect's third broad area of concern is the efficient management of a practice. A practice provides the architect with a base from which to offer services to clients. The strength and viability of this base, the practice, depends on sound business administration and management.

These three broad areas of concern for the content of practice—quality of services, professional responsibilities, and management of practice—are essentially the same for any professional in private practice, whether the practitioner's vocation is medicine, law, engineering, architecture, or another similar vocation rendering a personal service to the public. All of these concerns are necessary to succeed. However, the conditions under which an architect practices or renders services are somewhat different from those of other professionals.

The Conditions of Practice

To begin work, the architect signs a written agreement covering the services to be rendered to the client. The doctor, lawyer, or dentist rarely, if ever, enters into a written agreement to render professional services. Written agreements between an architect and the client are necessary and desirable for a number of reasons. The process of designing and constructing a building involves large sums of money and months of work, and original intents and objectives can become confused or lost entirely unless initially set down in writing. Further, building design and construction is an incredibly complicated process that is little understood by most clients. A written agreement clearly sets out for the client's benefit just what it is that is being stipulated and purchased.

Once the contract is signed, the architect depends on a vast array of diverse talents in rendering services. Obviously, no single person can be equally expert in architectural design as well as structural, mechanical, electrical, acoustical, landscape, and the dozens of other design disciplines involved in creating the typical contemporary building. Therefore, the architect depends on expert consultants in various areas of design entering into written agreements to cover their contributions to the project. However, the written agreement with the client ultimately means that the architect alone is responsible to the client for the quality of the design.

Other professionals may collaborate with related consultants to service their clients. A lawyer may suggest, for instance, that a client engage an insurance consultant, or a doctor may call in a specialist to consult on a particular problem. In most such situations, the consultant is engaged by and is responsible to the client; there is no written agreement between the primary professional and the consultant.

In designing a building, an architect deals with tremendous sums of construction money—other people's money. The architect's services determine how these sums are allocated to the various parts of the total building project. A relatively simple error on the architect's part—a misplaced dimension, for example—can be very costly to correct. While a doctor's or lawyer's error can lead to consequences beyond correction at any price, their services do not usually encompass as many diverse details and people, nor span such a lengthy period of time as do those of the architect, and, therefore, they are less exposed to chances for error than is the architect.

Finally, the architect depends upon an entirely separate party— the contractor—to enable him or her to complete the various services. During the building phase, the relationship between the architect and client changes somewhat from what it is during the design phase of the services. During the design phase, the architect's relationship to the client is often that of seller-buyer. During the construction phase, the architect traditionally becomes the client's representative—in effect, his or her agent—in all dealings with the contractor.

At the same time, the architect frequently is responsible for making decisions on claims instituted by both client and contractor. In making any decisions, the architect must be an impartial judge, favoring neither client nor contractor, and be interested only in seeing that the building project is completed in accordance with the requirements of the drawings, specifications, and other contract documents.

A large private developer may have an in-house staff of design professionals and legal professionals. The resulting responsibilities for the independent design firm may therefore vary drastically from the norm.

An awareness and appreciation of these concerns for the content and conditions of private architectural practice is vital to your understanding of the scope of architectural practice. They affect each of the architect's services and office activities, as you will see.

The Stages of a Design Project

An architect follows specific steps to ensure the proper completion of a design project. The various stages are described here.

Job Development

The architect's activities in private practice begin with job development by promoting services to potential clients; there will be no opportunity for the architect to practice if there are no clients.

The client will select a particular architect for a building project in one of a number of ways. The client may already know the architect socially or through some business contact, or may be familiar with the architect's work. If this is the case, the client may simply discuss the project with the architect, and the two parties will enter into an agreement to proceed with the required work. In other instances, the client may wish to review the qualifications and work of several architects, each of whom will discuss with the client several projects, completed or underway, that parallel the proposed project in function and size. They will each illustrate their respective qualifications to undertake the proposed work. Further, each architect may arrange for the client to visit the architect's office and one or more completed projects.

An architect may also be selected through a formal competition administered according to a detailed procedure outlined in the

American Institute of Architects' Code for Competitions. This selection procedure is usually used only in connection with large or particularly significant public projects.

In any event, the demands for a constant flow of work require the architect to be in daily contact with potential clients through personal participation in civic, social, professional, and business community activities. Maintaining these contacts also has the important result of educating the public about the function of the architect in the community. Even though a particular architect may not be selected for a project, he or she will nevertheless have rendered a real service to the public and to the profession by participating in the selection process.

Written Agreement

Once an architect has been selected for a project, he or she and the client execute a written owner-architect agreement that specifies the services the architect will render, the amount and method of compensation to the architect, and various other contractual details. Following execution of this agreement, the architect executes parallel agreements with consultants whose special services he or she has determined will be required on the proposed project. The drafting of agreements is the work of lawyers, and both architect and client consult with their respective legal counsels while negotiating the agreement.

Programming

The architect then begins planning the project. An initial step is programming all the activities that are to be housed in the building complex. The client, the architect, and the consultants all participate in developing the program. Also, contractors may be called in to advise on various construction problems uncovered during the discussion.

In brief terms, the program is a detailed description of all the functions to be included in the project and the square footage requirements for each. The program will clearly spell out relationships between the functions and any unique technical or mechanical requirements of each of the functions. It may also include preliminary cost figures, alternate structural and construction methods, materials to be considered, schedules and deadlines, and other items that are essential to the planning.

In essence, the program will cover every item of information the architect considers essential to the efficient execution of the design services. You can appreciate that the program will vary considerably among building types—a hospital as compared to an urban renewal project, for instance—and its quality will have a real effect upon the pace and smoothness of the entire design process.

Programming the project will reveal the need for certain owner-furnished information. The architect explains the need for this information to the client, who then arranges for it to be furnished by experts in the appropriate fields, or asks the architect to arrange for its preparation. The client will furnish information about the building site, including its size, boundaries, topography, utilities, easements, zoning, subsurface conditions, and existing buildings.

In addition to this basic site information, other special analyses may be necessary to properly program the project. For example, the client may be considering several types of projects or a variety of sites. Final determinations will then depend upon the findings of investigations of feasibility, market, financing, urban planning, land utilization, and zoning and site development.

Moreover, special functional requirements of the proposed project, for example, auditoriums, laboratories, or computer spaces, may require that special investigations be made of humidity, waste treatment, radiation shielding, and power supply before programming can be completed. Only when all necessary information has been gathered and collated can both client and architect approve the program; then the actual design can begin. Such special analyses will stretch out the programming phase of the architect's services.

Design

Actual design begins with the architect's preparation of schematic designs; these are the simple functional or space diagrams that illustrate an analysis of the project requirements as set out in the program. In preparing schematics, the architect's intuition as an artist alternates with his or her objective judgment as an engineer or scientist. Several solutions to the design problem may be developed and then presented to the client. These will be illustrated by simple line drawings showing the alternative solutions to problems of site development and volume and space interrelationships within and outside of the proposed structures. Brief written statements generally describing the solutions regarding overall design approach, structural and mechanical systems, materials, and probable costs will accompany the design schematics. The architect will, of course, recommend one solution above all others, but he or she may fully prepare alternative schematic solutions so that the client will gain the best possible understanding of the requirements of the project. A presentation is then made to the client, often employing the use of slides, simple perspectives, and models to secure the owner's approval of the best solution.

The approved schematic solution then enters the design development phase of the architect's services. Here it is the architect's objective to fix and illustrate the entire project in all its essentials. The materials prepared during this phase will form the basis for the construction documents and will determine the final form and character of the building. This phase of service is the heart of the architectural process, and full collaboration between the architect, client, and all of the special consultants is vital to the project's success.

Through this collaboration, the architect directs the preparation of drawings, outline specifications, cost statements, and other materials that may be required to provide a full understanding of the intended size, shape, and cost of the proposed project to all involved parties. Again, at the conclusion of this phase, the architect makes any presentations necessary in order to fully inform the client about the details of the project. In the case of public buildings, especially where bond referendums must be held to finance projects such as school buildings, the architect must make presentations at public hearings, zoning boards, and city or county councils. The architect will also want to participate in newspaper campaigns and other methods of public education when working on public buildings.

Construction Documents

When the design development materials are approved, the architect prepares the final construction documents. These include the working drawings and specifications that show or describe in detail all the work to be undertaken by the building contractors in the construction of the project. Their quality depends on the accuracy of cost estimates of the work and the effectiveness in constructing the building as the architect designed it. Thus, the architect and project consultants take special care to see that these documents are complete and accurate, so that they are understandable both in the offices of the architect and the contractor and at the project site in the midst of the construction.

The completed drawings (often fifty or more sheets, depending on the size and complexity of the project) are sent to the printer and the familiar blueprints are made from them. The specifications receive a final editing. Then they are printed and bound in a volume along with various bond and insurance forms, sample construction contracts, and similar contract documents prepared by the owner's legal and insurance counsel assisted by the architect. This volume will usually be hundreds of pages in length. A final, detailed cost estimate is usually made at this time to predict, as closely as possible, the actual price the contractor-bidders will quote for doing the work as designed and specified.

Bidding or Negotiation

The printed construction documents are then distributed to various construction contractors for their bidding or negotiation. The purpose of this phase of the architect's services is to select from among qualified contractors the one who will do the work shown and described in the document for the lowest dollar figure. It usually takes contractors about thirty days to assemble their figures, whereupon they each submit their own bid to the client. Generally, the qualified contractor who submits the lowest bid is selected by the client in consultation with the architect. An owner-contractor agreement covering the construction of the project is executed by the client and the selected contractor.

Construction may now begin. On many projects, the design process can take more than nine months from the day the client selects the architect to the day the contractor moves onto the construction site. This will vary, of course, with the size and complexity of the project. Also, on some projects, particularly manufacturing facilities, construction may start almost immediately after the first schematic designs are approved. Here the client, architect, and contractor are in constant collaboration. The architect designs, the client approves, and the contractor builds on a day-by-day, hour-by-hour schedule.

Construction Phase

During the construction phase, the architect provides general administration of the construction contract. The architect must check the bonds and insurance materials furnished by the contractor, check shop drawings and samples submitted by the contractor, and prepare any supplemental drawings or other interpretations required to clarify the construction documents. The architect then checks the results of specified tests, issues orders for any changes approved by the client, processes the contractor's billings to the client, checks required guarantees, and advises both client and contractor on the progress and quality of construction. The architect will issue a final certificate when all terms and conditions of the construction contract have been satisfactorily fulfilled.

During construction, the design becomes reality. If the contractor does not properly execute the construction work, a good share of the architect's months of design work can be wasted. Obviously the architect's management abilities are of prime importance, since administering construction contracts is crucial to the fulfillment of the design.

Construction of a commercial building can stretch from four months to two or more years, depending on the project's size, complexity, and weather conditions. The typical project probably takes twelve to eighteen months. Add this period to that required for design, and you will note that the architect will be engaged on each project for one to two years.

Postcompletion Services

When the construction of the project is complete, the client may wish to extend the original owner-architect agreement to include certain postcompletion services. These include continuing consultation on such issues as maintenance, repair, and remodeling. These services provide the client with expert counsel on how to secure the maximum usefulness of the building over its lifetime through maintenance and repair techniques that respond to the intent of the original design. Also, in rendering such services, the architect has an opportunity to study the performance of the design and to conduct on-site research in building maintenance and repair.

Expanding Architectural Services

We live in a period of great change. Probably no one feels this more strongly than you as a member of the generation about to take the first step in determining your life's work. You are constantly advised of the changes that are and will be taking place in every aspect of life and are further advised to properly evaluate the impact of these changed conditions on your choice of career. This advice is vital to the present and future practice of architecture.

At one time, architectural service included only the operations to be housed in a building, the availability of land on which to construct it, and the nature of its design and construction. The client simply told the architect that a building was needed to accommodate certain functions, that exactly so many dollars were available to spend on its design and construction, and that a certain piece of property was available on which the building was to be built. The architect then provided basic architectural services within these relatively simple limits. Now these limits are changing, and the architect must modify his or her services to respond to this change.

Some current examples of these changing limits will illustrate the scope of the change presently taking place.

New Kinds of Shelters Serve Today's New Functions

- The subdivision is more common than the individual home.
- The development complex is replacing the subdivision.
- The shopping mall is replacing the isolated store building.

Rehabilitation and Conversion of Old Buildings to New Uses Is Replacing New Construction in Some Areas

- The use of computers, the Internet, and DVDs in the classroom are replacing traditional teaching methods.
- Catalog and Internet sales are replacing store purchases at point-of-sale.
- Telecommunication is shrinking office space and transforming office space usage.

Availability of Land on Which to Place the Building Has Changed

- Less and less open land is available for construction.
- Relocation and demolition may frequently precede new construction.
- Zoning and other land-use regulations increasingly dictate what can be built and where it can be built.
- Placement of traffic and transportation facilities have a dramatic effect on the most appropriate and efficient use of land resources.

Financing and Cost of Constructing the Building Has Changed

- Projects are generally larger in scope (the shopping mall versus the store) and require larger sums of money.

- Certain commercial interests, such as the insurance industry, have tremendous sums of money available for long-term investments, such as building. At the same time, the typical client, a manufacturer for instance, wants to retain company funds for purchase of equipment and materials required in manufacturing operations. Thus institutions like insurance companies are increasingly becoming a second "client," since they will own the building upon its completion and will lease it to a tenant, such as a manufacturer.
- Federal agency programs of subsidy, grants-in-aids, loans, and mortgage guaranty firms in certain construction fields may bring a third "client" into the building project.
- Economic cycles of inflation/recession and rising costs in financing, construction, and maintenance in all areas require greater ingenuity to produce cost-effective and energy-effective buildings.

These are but a few examples of the changes taking place in our time that affect the architect's services. Many more could be noted, but they all point to the fact that changing times have created conditions in which early, predesign decisions on how operations are to be housed, how land is to be assembled, and how construction is to be financed, will increasingly dictate the final architectural design. If the architect is not involved in these decisions, the project's design will be dictated by decisions that were developed previously by others.

The architectural profession is responding to these changes by expanding basic services to match the requirements of our changing times. Some firms combine the resources of outside experts with their own talents to perform expanded services. Other firms frequently enter into a joint venture or join an association with two or more firms to provide a package of services that a single firm, acting alone, would not be able to provide. In any event, it is evident that these expanded services are becoming standard services of the architect.

Here are some of the expanded services now being offered more and more frequently by the average architectural practice.

Project Analysis Services
Building condition assessment
Feasibility analysis
Financial analysis
Location and site analysis
Zoning and building code analysis
Market and merchandising analysis
Operational programming analysis
Building programming analysis

Promotional Services
Real estate and land assembly
Project development and financing
Promotional design and planning
Public relations

Design and Planning Services
Program development
Urban and regional planning
Civil engineering—traffic, transit, roads, sanitary
Landscape architecture and site development
Building design
Structural engineering

Mechanical engineering
Electrical engineering
Interior design and equipment planning
Fine arts
Architectural graphics
Special design analysis—acoustics, lighting
Cost analysis
Drawing and specifications

Construction Services
Bidding and negotiation of contracts
Administration of contracts
Job cost accounting
Construction management
Postconstruction services

Related Services
Consultation on operational programming and building
Programming in specific building types
Research and testing
Product development and design
Consultation on building product manufacturing and
    prefabrication processes

Payment for Services

The architect's fee for professional services varies as in any other
profession. It depends on the architect's standing in the field, the
geographic location in which the architect practices, and the type
of project undertaken. However, one aspect of the architect's com-

pensation remains the same throughout the profession: the architect's only remuneration is that received from the client. The architect does not accept any commission or discounts on materials, equipment, labor costs, or any other item involved in project cost. This arrangement makes it clear that the architect's loyalty is to the client and to the project.

The amount of the architect's fee and method of payment are settled at the time the owner-architect agreement is executed. There are five principal methods of compensating the architect, although others may be agreed upon:

- A percentage of the project's construction cost
- A multiple of the architect's direct personnel expense
- A professional fee plus the reimbursement of the architect's expenses
- A lump sum fee
- A salary, per diem, or hourly compensation

The percentage method is the most popular simply because it is the most convenient to compute, it is tied directly to the construction cost, and it provides the client with a firm idea of what will have to be paid for the architect's total basic services. However, the convenience of the percentage fee depends on a clear definition of basic services.

As these services include more and more of the expanded services discussed above—most of which involve research and investigation and, therefore, cannot be precisely estimated in terms of time and cost—the percentage fee system is bound to fall from general usage. Many architects believe it will be replaced by a combination system where compensation for services would be computed as follows:

- **Programming, schematics, and design development.**
  Professional fee plus expenses, or multiple of the direct
  personnel expense fee
- **Construction documents.** Lump sum fee
- **Bidding or negotiation.** Hourly fee
- **Contract administration.** Professional fee plus expenses or
  multiple of direct personnel expense
- **Postcompletion.** Hourly fee
- **Other services.** Professional fee plus expenses, or multiple of
  direct personnel expense

Based on general trends, a combination system of this sort will be
generally employed by the profession when you enter practice some
six to eight years from now.

The Architect's Office

Every office that performs architectural services has the word *architect* written on the door. Somewhere behind that door is an individual who uses this word after his or her name and who is legally
authorized to use an architect's stamp on construction documents.
That is where the similarity among offices ends.

The office may contain a sole practitioner or more than two hundred people. If the office is in New England, the Pacific North-
west, or the Pacific Southwest, it is highly probable that the office
will contain a sole practitioner. In the East North Central and East
South Central United States, it is highly likely that the office will
contain a firm of twenty or more employees. The AIA regularly
publishes statistics about its membership. Over 50 percent of the
member firms employ fewer than five people. Over 90 percent of
the firms employ fewer than twenty people. There are fewer than

twenty firms in the United States with more than one hundred architect employees. These kinds of statistics also hold true in many major industrialized nations around the world.

The size of the firm often determines what kinds of work the firm can seek. Private individual clients are more likely to choose a smaller firm. The state and federal government, institutions, and large industrial clients tend to work with large firms. Firms of all sizes work with developers.

It is virtually impossible to know at the outset of an architectural career what kind of office to prepare for. As a rule of thumb, many people who begin in small offices seem to finish their careers in large firms. Those who start out in large firms often open their own small firms in the latter years of their careers. Most people begin a career in any design field having primarily an artistic or work satisfaction motivation. Later in their careers, economic motivation often becomes a more dominant goal, sometimes as the result of a growing family.

Every career involves the balance of these important issues. There is no question that compensation for the same level of employment is greater in a large firm. A principal in a large firm can make twice the annual salary of a sole practitioner. Even interns in a large firm earn more than small-firm interns, although the difference may be only 10 or 12 percent.

It is very important to understand that the work done by employees of a small firm is quite different from that done in a very large firm. The most important difference is specialization. Generally speaking, in a small firm everyone is expected to do more of everything. If the office receives an important job that requires extensive work, everyone may switch for a time to that project. One day is spent drafting, the next day may require model building, and the day after could be spent on writing specifications. In a large firm, it is much more likely that the work will be more specialized. Draftspeople may never write a specification or visit a construction site. A designer may also spend a large portion of his or her career on a specific type of building. If variety becomes important, moving to another firm may be necessary.

Sole practitioners are dependent upon others for expertise they do not have. One could say that small practitioners have the largest offices, namely the rest of the community. If a bigger job comes to a small office, the architect may hire a few people for a brief time or contract out the work. The essence of success for a small firm is the ability to diversify. If the market slows down in one area, it moves to another. Small offices find stability in repeat work. The more work done with the same client, the less time consumed in marketing services and customizing work methods and the greater the profit margin. Developers with repeat projects are good clients for a small office.

Life in a large firm is more social, and in many ways it is a direct extension of architectural school. Three or four people may lunch together regularly. Work is frequently done by a team. The Christmas party is often the social highlight of the year. The whole office may go to a baseball game or a picnic in the summer.

The structure of the social environment is also demanding in a large firm. Generally speaking, working in a large firm means climbing the corporate ladder. Employees start at the bottom and work to the top. The lowest level is that of draftsperson or model maker. With experience, the draftsperson becomes a project architect responsible for a specific building design and working directly with the client or the client's representatives. With more experience, the employee assumes the role of project manager with several project architects to supervise. Above the project managers are the senior-level firm associates with overall responsibility for the work the firm performs. Finally, there is the principal/partner who owns part or all of the firm and has major financial responsibility and firm leadership duties, as well as the task of seeking and serving clients. Climbing this ladder in an office obviously takes both architectural experience and good social and political skills. The people at the highest levels of the firm frequently are also accomplished in the financial skills necessary to maintain a business.

The person who owns a small firm and the person who owns a large firm are probably not doing the same job each day. The sole practitioner may still be doing drafting and have major design responsibility for an admittedly small building. The person in charge of a large firm may spend most of the week in a boardroom and may never pick up a pencil. One person could be responsible for $2 million in building costs per year, the other may oversee projects worth $200 million. One person may be solving a problem about a board and a nail, while the other may be meeting with the board of a corporation to resolve a master plan. These two architects may have been college classmates or taken the same Architect Registration Exam.

Present and Future Practice

Changing times have had their effect on the architect's services. Yet the ultimate objectives and functions of architectural practice remain what they have always been: to design buildings, and the spaces between them, and to administrate contracts for their construction. But the methods of practice are becoming very different from those traditionally employed to reach these objectives.

In June 1998 the American Institute of Architects (AIA) appointed a task force to develop a long-range plan. It was charged with "Aligning the Institute for the Millennium" and subsequently became known as the AIM Task Force. Its product was the *AIM Report*, and its mission was to, ". . . challenge the comfortable assumptions in order to look into the future for where the profession will be, or needs to be, and to determine how the Institute can best support the growth and success of the profession."

The *AIM Report* itself is available upon request from the AIA. The major objectives that were identified by the task force are summarized here:

- **Architecture education.** Promote the accountability of schools offering professional degree programs in architecture for better preparing their students to become architects upon graduation
- **Information and knowledge delivery.** Identify and provide market-driven, timely, relevant, concise, and accessible information and knowledge, using all appropriate delivery systems
- **External dialogue.** Seek opportunities and create mechanisms to foster dialogue that engages the architect with the marketplace
- **Partners.** Identify, promote, and enhance strategic partnerships between members, their clients, and other contributors to the built environment
- **Advocacy.** Initiate and enable results-oriented advocacy with government and industry at the state, local, and national levels, speaking with a clear and consistent voice
- **Inclusiveness.** Aggressively broaden the membership base to be more inclusive, and focus services to anticipate and creatively respond to member needs
- **Governance.** Transform the culture, structure, and resources of the institute to facilitate the bold implications of policies

that support the (AIM) mission and (AIM) vision statements and provide more timely, consistent, and innovative responses to emerging issues.

Your Practice

This concludes our discussion of the details of architectural practice as we know it today. The next chapter discusses the education and licensing requirements you must meet before you can enter the community as an architect.

Chances are that when you enter your own practice, you will be a person with quite different qualifications from those of today's architect, for the expanded services and new techniques of practice discussed in this chapter will radically affect architectural education and practice in your time. These changes are bound to multiply at an ever-increasing rate. Such is the nature of the computerized society in which we live.

As important as these changes will be to your practice as an architect and to your responsibility for continuing self-education as a professional, they will not in any way alter the basic architectural mission—the creation of humanity's physical environment. Rather, the changes will broaden your practice by freeing you of much of the handwork now associated with research, analysis, and computation, thus affording you greater control over management and design processes and permitting you to spend more time on creative design.

6

EDUCATION FOR ARCHITECTURE

YOUR ELEMENTARY AND secondary education form the foundation for your education toward a professional career. They had much to do with your decision to consider a selected number of possible career options from among the thousands available in today's economy. You are now ready to select a formal course of instruction that will prepare you for your occupation. It is an extremely important consideration, for your commitment to your education will be extraordinary in terms of both financial investment and intellectual dedication.

You have begun your selection early in your schooling by choosing certain courses in junior and senior high school. Thereafter you will invest five to eight years of your life and anywhere from $5,000 to $30,000 per year for your college education.

In light of these considerable investments, it makes good sense that you have a firm insight into the challenges and opportunities offered by a career in architecture, that you make a candid appraisal of your attitudes and abilities, and that you gain a broad understanding of the educational and licensing requirements you must satisfy to enter the profession.

This chapter discusses these educational and licensing requirements and the tuition and other costs associated with them. Before we proceed, however, we should briefly review careers in architecture and the attitudes required of those who choose to enter the profession and vocation of architecture.

The Construction Industry

As an architect, your work will be combined with that of many other disciplines in the construction industry—urban planning, engineering, education, contracting and financing, to name just a few. Your contribution to the process of creating buildings will be one of leadership, and your decisions will put these other disciplines into action.

As you pursue your career, you may discover that one or more of these other disciplines are as attractive to you as architecture. If so, you will further find that your basic education and training in architecture have prepared you to move with competence into these other disciplines with a relatively small amount of additional education and/or training.

The work of the architect is cyclical, partly because of the nature of construction, but it is determined more by the nature of the client or buying public. A client may speculate for some time on whether to build, but once having decided, he or she is anxious to see the project completed. Therefore, for most projects, the architect is obliged to be patient while the client is making a decision and then to bring all available resources to bear on completing the project as soon as possible following the client's favorable decision. Deadlines, overtime, and evening work are commonplace for the architect.

Professional Choices

The architect is a professional and, as such, holds a primary concern for people—for their health, their safety, and their general welfare. The architect reveals this concern by exercising judgment in solving the client's building problems. These decisions are as often based on moral and technical issues as on the monetary issues involved. This philosophy of service to others before self demands a dedication to certain ideals easily overlooked in the pressures of today's materialistic society. The opportunity for intrinsic rewards is immense: the satisfaction of exercising independent judgment, the joy of creation, the appreciation of those served, the recognition by others of your professional achievements.

Those trained in architecture need not confine their talents to design. A career in architecture offers opportunities in sales, technical writing, contract law, administration, business and personnel management, cost accounting, computer science, and many other disciplines in addition to design. Within the practice of architecture, there are as many career opportunities as can be found in almost any other discipline. It merely remains for you to determine which turn you wish your career to take. This determination rests primarily upon your own attitudes and aptitudes.

Review of Attitudes and Aptitudes

Now that you are aware of the various challenges, opportunities, and rewards of architecture, perhaps you should review the list of character traits needed to become an architect (see Chapter 3). How do your own characteristics measure up to the requirements of the profession?

Your assets for a successful career in architecture include the ability to work under pressure and with all kinds of people. You are prepared to devote the necessary years to your education and understand that intrinsic rewards will sometimes be your greater satisfaction. You are creative, enthusiastic, and have a good artistic sense. You exercise sound judgment and can deal with others diplomatically while maintaining a sense of propriety. You can manage a variety of details and have the perseverance to stay with a project despite delays and other pressures. Finally, you possess the technological, communications, and management skills necessary for success in any profession.

As improbable as it may seem, the truly successful professional architect exhibits all these characteristics. To be sure, some were developed following formal education, but the aptitudes were there all the time waiting to be revealed by the demands of a professional career. The earlier they are revealed, the earlier you will know the satisfaction of matching your attitudes and aptitudes to the challenges and opportunities of a career in architecture.

Preparation While in High School

The education and experience that are necessary for a career in architecture are acquired in stages. The process begins with your choice of an architectural career and proceeds through your formal schooling, internship, licensure, and professional years. Once started, the process never really stops.

Formal schooling and internship, from secondary school to licensure, will usually consume from eight to ten years. This allows for five to seven years of professional study and three to four years of internship. While this process cannot be appreciably accelerated, even for the gifted student, it can be made more meaningful and productive by an early career decision. If you make your career decision early in your secondary school years, you will tend to focus your attention on those junior and senior high school courses and activities that stimulate the talents and interests vital to a successful architect.

As you approach your decision to pursue an architectural career, consult your school's vocational guidance counselor. The counselor will assist you in making this early decision by helping you identify your talents and motivations, matching these against the requirements of the profession, and suggesting secondary school courses and extracurricular activities that will strengthen your overall capabilities. Later in your secondary education, the counselor will focus your attention on those colleges and universities offering courses in architectural education that most nearly match your particular interests and capabilities.

Among the most important skills required in architectural education and practice are the ability to communicate and a capacity for scientific reasoning. Consequently, artistic, linguistic, mathematic, and scientific skills are important prerequisites to a college architectural curriculum. Your aptitude in these areas should be identified and developed as early as possible.

Specific entrance requirements vary from college to college. Certain guidelines may be mentioned, but you must always check the requirements of a particular school. General guidelines include graduation from an accredited high school, with rank in the upper one-third or one-fourth of the graduating class or, in some cases, with a B average, and fifteen or sixteen units total in the following subject areas:

English, 3–4 units
Mathematics, 3–4 units
Science, 2–3 units
Social studies, 1–2 units

Foreign language, 1–2 units
Other (history, economics, other appropriate electives),
    1–2 units

In addition to your secondary school academic record, you may be required to submit certain other materials, including:

- Record of Scholastic Aptitude Test and other specialized tests of the College Entrance Examination Board (CEEB) administered by the Educational Testing Service (ETS). Visit www.collegeboard.com or www.ets.org for information. Some schools also will accept test scores from the American College Testing Program (ACT), www.act.org.
- Recommendation of school principal and other qualified persons
- Health record
- Evidence of personal qualities, educational and career objectives, basic skills in visual arts
- Record of any special tests administered by the particular school to which you are applying

These add up to a most impressive set of academic and extracurricular requirements. They emphasize the value of an early decision on a career and an early investigation of the precise requirements of the particular school you choose. Again, you should discuss these matters with your school's vocational counselor early in your secondary schooling. The counselor will have many suggestions on how you should shape your secondary school activities to prepare for college admission. Although it is the rare eighth-grader who is actively preparing for his or her career at such an early age, the decision process might be started then.

Whenever you begin, the first step is to consider two or three careers that interest you, including architecture. Then you need to research which colleges offer the best training in these fields. If possible, you should match your academic and extracurricular choices to the admissions requirements at those schools. Closer to the date of your graduation, you will need to narrow your choices of schools and begin visiting college campuses in person to select the one that will best meet your needs.

In implementing your educational plan, you must remember two principal points. First, be sure to contact the colleges you are interested in, take the required tests, and gather any necessary information. Your guidance counselor can advise you on these matters, but it is up to you to carry them out. Second, most arrangements must be made months in advance. For instance, many college admissions applications must be submitted in February for September matriculation.

Do not be overly concerned if your preparation thus far has not followed a specific route intended to result in a career in architecture. Many people do not establish their career goals until much later in college or even after graduation. For any important voyage, however, once you know where you want to go, it always helps to have a map. Once you commit your life to being an architect, you can say you are one. However, it takes some very specific steps to convince the rest of the world to allow you to practice your chosen profession.

To skip college is not in your best interest professionally or financially. Likewise, merely attending any available college is a luxury you cannot afford. When you enter a course of instruction, it should be with the full expectation that you can meet its required level of performance as well as manage its costs. Therefore, choosing the college program that is best suited to you is extremely important.

This may mean that you should start in a junior college or small liberal arts college, later moving on to a larger university for your professional work. Or, you may find that your first years are best spent in a college in your hometown where you can live at home, saving up for the last years at a more distant school. In any event, the choice is not just a school or combination of schools, but a total undergraduate and professional educational program that will meet your particular needs.

In searching for the academic program that is best for you, there are three groups of factors you should consider. The first focuses on you:

- **How good a student are you?** If you are in the top 10 percent of the class, your choice of colleges is largely unlimited. Below this, your choice is somewhat restricted. This is to your benefit, for if you entered a school having higher performance requirements than you can match, you might soon be buried under an impossible academic load.
- **What kind of school is best for you?** Are you prepared to go immediately into a college curriculum that leads directly to a professional degree in architecture, or should you spend the first years in a liberal arts college?
- **What size school is best for you?** The relative advantages and disadvantages of large and small schools are obvious but often are not adequately considered by many young people.

While you areconsidering these questions, don't forget you have three excellent resources at hand to advise you: your parents and/or other adult family members and friends, your school's vocational guidance counselor, and anyone you know who is currently in his or her final undergraduate or early graduate years. Your friends who are currently completing their college work have the freshest possible view on what it is like to attend today's college or university.

The second group of factors to consider in choosing a school focuses on the college:

- **Are the school's architectural programs accredited by the National Architectural Accrediting Board (NAAB)?** If its programs are not accredited, the school's graduates may receive only partial credit toward those academic requirements needed to apply for licensing examinations in most states. The types of programs offered by schools accredited by NAAB are not necessarily identical. In fact, they may vary considerably from school to school. As you plan your visits to various schools, you will want to brief yourself ahead of time on the program choices. Such information can be obtained by contacting each school separately or by securing a copy of the publication *Guide to Architecture Schools*. This annual publication can be ordered from the Association of Collegiate Schools of Architecture at www.acsa-arch.org/store. This is a very complete collection of information that will brief you on almost every question you may want to ask when you visit schools.
- **What are the specific admission and degree requirements of the school, and what does the school have to offer?** What requirements must you meet to earn your degree in architecture? What is the content of the required and elective courses? What level degree will you earn? How many years will it take? How large is the college student body? What are the qualifications of its faculty? What kind of physical

facilities are available both for academic work and for residence? These facts are related in the catalog and website of each college. Also, they are briefed in the statistical information publication available from the Association of Collegiate Schools of Architecture at the website noted above.

Your best source of guidance in discussing any college is the college itself. If possible, plan to visit the schools of your choice and talk directly with their admissions officers and with the faculty members responsible for interviewing potential applicants. Recent graduates are also good resources. Older alumni can be helpful even though most colleges have changed considerably in the last decade. Of course, your guidance counselor is usually your first source of information and your best overall adviser in comparing facts gathered from a group of schools in which you may be interested.

The third group of factors to consider focuses on costs:

- **What does the school cost, and how will you pay for tuition?** What are the tuition costs and other fees for resident students? For nonresident students? What is covered by tuition payments? By fees? When are they payable? What are the estimates of the cost of room and board? Are scholarships available? Jobs on campus? Is this a work-study program school?
- **Have you considered travel costs to and from home and college?** Will you need to finance your education through loans such as personal, college, private organization, or government loan?

Actual dollar costs for tuition, fees, room, board, travel, and incidental expenses vary considerably throughout the over one hundred architectural schools in the United States and Canada. However, we can offer some guidelines:

- **State-supported school in your home state.** Budget at least $5,000 to $8,000 per year plus travel.
- **State-supported school outside your home state.** Budget at least $10,000 to $15,000 per year plus travel.
- **Private school.** Budget at least $10,000 to $30,000 per year plus travel.

After bringing together all the costs associated with each school you are considering, you should make out a tentative budget covering the full college period and detail as accurately as possible the first two years. Only then will you appreciate the considerable investment you are about to make in your education. Colleges often assist students in outlining a complete financing program. Also, your parents and your school's vocational guidance counselor will be of vital assistance here.

Student Financial Aid

There are many sources of financial aid and scholarships available to the serious college student. Your guidance counselor will have information on sources and applicant qualifications.

The U.S. Department of Education maintains a website through which you can apply for federal financial aid. The site is called Free Application for Federal Student Aid, and it can be accessed at www.fafsa.ed.gov. Another useful website is www.finaid.org, which offers extensive information on loans, scholarships, and other forms of aid.

A number of other popular financing and scholarship references are available through your local bookstore or library. Some such publications cover scholarships exclusively. Further information on this subject is frequently found in appendixes to various college directories published annually and available through retail book outlets.

The American Institute of Architects administers a variety of scholarship programs, and these are available to architecture students on an annual basis. Details of these and other AIA scholarships may be secured by writing to the Director of Educational Programs, The American Institute of Architects, 1735 New York Avenue NW, Washington, DC 20006-5292. You can also visit the AIA's website at www.aia.org/ed_default.

If you are serious about applying for financial assistance or scholarships, it is important to remember that most such awards are given in the spring (usually in April) for the following fall semester. Therefore, applications usually must be filed the previous December through February. To gather all the necessary information, it is important that you begin your search for available funding several months prior to these deadlines, or at least a year before the funding will be needed.

The School Also Chooses You

Earlier we discussed the attitudes and aptitudes necessary to be a professional architect. Obviously similar attributes are important to a school seeking applicants to its program. However, since schools don't mistake the decision to enter an architectural program with the decision to enter the profession, you should not confuse the two either. You are allowed to use school as a trial run. Concentrate on the task at hand: successful application and admission to a school of architecture.

Generally speaking, academic programs are looking for students who demonstrate a good balance of analytical and creative skills. Early inspiration to be an architect tends to emphasize aesthetics. As a student matures into an architect, the aesthetic ability is assured and learning the rudiments of building and engineering science play a greater role. Ultimately, all of the professional basics must be mastered to obtain registration. Without a reasonably solid foundation in math and science, you will be crippled from the outset in architectural school. Schools understand that fact.

Computer graphics and drafting have become a fact of life in architectural offices and, therefore, are also a primary component of architectural curricula. Schools note and appreciate existing computer literacy and skills.

Architectural schools are also looking for students with talent. Someone once said that talent is the ability to do easily what others find difficult. The corollary is also true: genius is the ability to do easily what the talented find difficult. Talent cannot be acquired, but it can be developed.

When you enter a school of architecture, you will find that all of your colleagues are also talented, but perhaps in different ways. It is the competitive academic environment that will cause you to develop your talent. Good schools admit those candidates whom they perceive are the most talented, and they hope the talented are also willing to work hard.

As discussed earlier, if you want to be an architect you must remain an eternal student. If you are successful, larger and larger commissions will come your way. Be sure to learn from your failures as well as your successes. Ultimately, you will be competing with the people of genius throughout history. Only a handful of architects in each generation can claim a place among them.

College Course Work

Earlier in this chapter we gave certain guidelines on college admission requirements. Here we present some guidelines concerning the curriculum offered. Again, we emphasize that these are general guidelines only and that you must always check the course content of the particular school of your choice.

The NAAB only accredits five-year bachelor of architecture programs and the master of architecture degrees programs. There are no four-year accredited undergraduate programs in architecture. The curricular requirements for awarding these degrees must include three components: general studies, professional studies, and electives.

These components are defined by NAAB as follows:

- **General studies.** Students must complete coursework in the arts and sciences. These general studies are a prerequisite to pursuing a professional degree.
- **Professional studies.** At minimum, any professional program must include the courses required by the NAAB Student Performance Criteria, as well as any additional courses as dictated by the educational institution.
- **Electives.** To ensure a well-rounded education, students should be able to pursue special interests in the form of minors or develop other areas of concentration, either within or outside the program, as they work toward a professional degree.

The electives respond to the institutional needs, the needs of the profession, and the needs of the individual students. All of these components together define a liberal education in architecture.

For the purposes of NAAB accreditation, graduating students must demonstrate awareness, understanding, or ability in the following areas:

1. **Verbal and writing skills.** Ability to speak and write effectively on subject matter contained in the professional curriculum
2. **Graphic skills.** Ability to employ appropriate representational media, including computer technology, to convey essential formal elements at each stage of the programming and design process
3. **Research skills.** Ability to employ basic methods of data collection and analysis to inform all aspects of the programming and design process
4. **Critical thinking skills.** Ability to make a comprehensive analysis and evaluation of a building, building complex, or urban space
5. **Fundamental design skills.** Ability to apply basic organizational, spatial, structural, and constructional principles to the conception and development of interior and exterior spaces, building elements, and components
6. **Collaborative skills.** Ability to identify and assume divergent roles that maximize individual talents and to cooperate with other students when working as members of a design team and in other settings
7. **Human behavior.** Awareness of the theories and methods of inquiry that seek to clarify the relationships between human behavior and the physical environment
8. **Human diversity.** Awareness of the diversity of needs, values, behavioral norms, and social and spatial patterns that characterize different cultures, and the implications of

this diversity for the societal roles and responsibilities of
architects

9. **Use of precedents.** Ability to provide a coherent rationale
for the programmatic and formal precedents employed in
the conceptualization and development of architecture and
urban design projects

10. **Western traditions.** Understanding of the Western
architectural canons and traditions in architecture,
landscape, and urban design, as well as the climatic,
technological, socioeconomic, and other cultural factors
that have shaped and sustained them

11. **Nonwestern traditions.** Awareness of the parallel and
divergent canons and traditions of architecture and urban
design in the non-Western world

12. **National and regional traditions.** Understanding of the
national traditions and the local regional heritage in
architecture, landscape, and urban design, including
vernacular traditions

13. **Environmental conservation.** Understanding of the basic
principles of ecology and architects' responsibilities with
respect to environmental and resource conservation in
architecture and urban design

14. **Accessibility.** Ability to design both site and building to
accommodate individuals with varying physical abilities

15. **Site conditions.** Ability to respond to natural and built site
characteristics in the development of a program and design
of a project

16. **Formal ordering systems.** Understanding of the
fundamentals of visual perception and the principles and
systems of order that inform two- and three-dimensional
design, architectural composition, and urban design

17. **Structural systems.** Understanding of the principles of structural behavior in withstanding gravity and lateral forces, and the evolution, range, and appropriate applications of contemporary structural systems

18. **Environmental systems.** Understanding of the basic principles that inform the design of environmental systems, including acoustics, lighting and climate modification systems, and energy use

19. **Life-safety systems.** Understanding of the basic principles that inform the design and selection of life-safety systems in buildings and their subsystems

20. **Building envelope systems.** Understanding of the basic principles that inform the design of building envelope systems

21. **Building service systems.** Understanding of the basic principles that inform the design of building service systems, including plumbing, electrical, vertical transportation, communication, security, and fire protection systems

22. **Building systems integration.** Ability to assess, select, and integrate structural systems, environmental systems, life-safety systems, building envelope systems, and building service systems into building design

23. **Legal responsibilities.** Understanding of architects' legal responsibilities with respect to public health, safety, and welfare; property rights; zoning and subdivision ordinances; building codes; accessibility and other factors affecting building design, construction, and architecture practice

24. **Building code compliance.** Understanding of the codes, regulations, and standards applicable to a given site and

building design, including occupancy classifications, allowable building heights and areas, allowable construction types, separation requirements, occupancy requirements, means of egress, fire protection, and structure

25. **Building materials and assemblies.** Understanding of the principles, conventions, standards, applications, and restrictions pertaining to the manufacture and use of construction materials, components, and assemblies

26. **Building economics and cost control.** Awareness of the fundamentals of development financing, building economics, and construction cost control within the framework of a design project

27. **Detailed design development.** Ability to assess, select, configure, and detail as an integral part of the design appropriate combinations of building materials, components, and assemblies to satisfy the requirements of building programs

28. **Technical documentation.** Ability to make technically precise descriptions and documentation of a proposed design for purposes of review and construction

29. **Comprehensive design.** Ability to produce an architecture project informed by a comprehensive program, from schematic design through the detailed development of programmatic spaces, structural and environmental systems, life-safety provisions, wall sections, and building assemblies, as may be appropriate; and to assess the completed project with respect to the program's design criteria

30. **Program preparation.** Ability to assemble a comprehensive program for an architectural project,

including an assessment of client and user needs, a critical review of appropriate precedents, an inventory of space and equipment requirements, an analysis of site conditions, a review of the relevant laws and standards and an assessmentof their implications for the project, and a definition of site selection and design assessment criteria

31. **The legal context of architecture practice.** Awareness of the evolving legal context within which architects practice, and of the laws pertaining to professional registration, professional service contracts, and the formation of design firms and related legal entities

32. **Practice organization and management.** Awareness of the basic principles of office organization, business planning, marketing, negotiation, financial management, and leadership, as they apply to the practice of architecture

33. **Contracts and documentation.** Awareness of the different methods of project delivery, the corresponding forms of service contracts, and the types of documentation required to render competent and responsible professional service

34. **Professional internship.** Understanding of the role of internship in professional development, and the reciprocal rights and responsibilities of interns and employers

35. **Architects' leadership roles.** Awareness of architects' leadership roles from project inception, design, and design development to contract administration, including the selection and coordination of allied disciplines, postoccupancy evaluation, and facility management

36. **The context of architecture.** Understanding of the shifts that occur—and have occurred—in the social, political, technological, ecological, and economic factors that shape the practice of architecture

37. **Ethics and professional judgment.** Awareness of the
ethical issues involved in the formation of professional
judgments in architecture design and practice

As already mentioned, architectural programs vary from school
to school. Some schools offer subjects in four-year courses leading
to a bachelor of arts degree (B.A.), with two additional years to earn
a master of architecture (M.Arch.). Other schools offer a more concentrated five-year course leading to a bachelor of architecture
(B.Arch.). A few schools offer a bachelor of science (B.S.) in architecture degree earned after four years of formal courses. Depending on the content of the undergraduate courses, the master's degree
could take as long as seven years. Check each college's course information closely to be sure that you understand its content and length
and know whether the school and its degrees are fully accredited
by the NAAB. A degree from an accredited school of architecture
is usually a requirement to be eligible for registration.

College admissions is a big business. Each year one to two million high school graduates apply for admission to our nation's colleges and universities. Some schools will receive many thousands of
applications, and they are able to enroll less than 10 percent of those
who apply. You can get a head start on this process and avoid many
of the tensions associated with it if you follow the suggestions we
have discussed here while you are in secondary school and choosing your college architectural program. It is up to you to start the
process and to keep it moving once it is under way.

The College Experience

Many of your experiences as a student in an architectural curriculum will be similar to those of college students in other curricula.

However, there are a few unique experiences in an architectural program, and you will be interested to know of them and what they entail.

For instance, laboratory courses are common to the architectural curriculum. The architectural student's principal laboratory is the drafting room and the art studio for courses in composition and design, drawing and sketching, drafting and presentation, and painting and sculpture. All of these activities involve a great deal of experimentation in the materials and techniques of the visual arts and consume great chunks of a student's time. Because of the equipment involved—drafting boards, computers, and a sizable quantity of paper, paints, and other materials—almost all of this lab work is done at school. In most schools, the labs are open all night, as the students in architecture push to meet a morning deadline.

Since much of the student's work is done in visual media, there is a great deal of brainstorming, kibitzing, and criticism of each other's work. Free advice is always in great supply at any art or architectural school. Consequently, open competition along with a full exchange of ideas is characteristic of architectural schools. Out of this grows a great camaraderie among the students. Traditionally, confrontations, discussions, debates, and occasionally comic relief through a healthy amount of practical joking are hallmarks of the architectural school.

The talents of architectural students lend themselves admirably to the creation, design, and preparation of graphics, stagecraft, layouts for school publications, decorations, and constructions for various campus happenings. The architectural student never wants for involvement in extracurricular activities. The biggest problem may well be avoiding overextending yourself, for the architectural curriculum is normally so demanding that very little time remains to devote to nonacademic pursuits.

The student of architecture should have no problem finding summer employment that will offer personal and career development. The most valuable summer employment puts the student in direct contact with the building process: clerking in a building supply outlet or even a general hardware store, working as an assistant on a surveying team, working for a general or mechanical contractor, serving as an office helper/assistant in an architect's or engineer's office, or working for any of the thousands of retail, wholesale, or manufacturing businesses that serve the building industry, including blueprint shops, brick and masonry yards, and lumber mills.

Architecture is tangible. It is best understood when seen, felt, and experienced firsthand. Therefore, travel is an essential part of an architect's education. Personal finances may not allow a trip around the United States, Canada, Mexico, or other countries until well after your graduation, but you should plan to travel as much as possible and as early in your career as finances will permit. While in school, you will take field trips under school sponsorship; you may even be fortunate enough to be awarded a scholarship just for travel. In the meantime, you have your own hometown, the city in which the college is located, and all the points in between. Moreover, every region in the United States has something to be seen that will be of value to your architectural education. Make these your travel objectives for the moment.

It is characteristic of the architect to be minutely observant of all surroundings, and you should begin now to train yourself to really see everything you look at—both natural and constructed objects—analyzing each for its function, its materials, its structure, and its relationship to other things.

During your third year of college, you will need to give serious attention to the possibility of attending graduate school. Historically, the architect completed the required formal education with a bachelor's degree, but this has changed. The qualified student is encouraged to very seriously consider courses to earn a master's degree in architecture, structural engineering, or urban planning. Another possibility might be earning a second bachelor's degree in a field related to architecture and construction, such as landscape architecture; civil, electrical, or mechanical engineering; law; economics; or business administration. As has been repeatedly pointed out in this book, the architect's field of interest is broadening to include every activity that affects our physical environment. This broadening interest requires leadership from those trained in multiple disciplines. If you have the basic qualifications for this leadership, it would be wise for you to train for this role by earning a graduate degree.

Your Training as an Intern

Employment both during school and after graduation means a great deal more than an opportunity to earn a living. Your first job is also your first step in fulfilling the period of internship required by your state registration board. Usually three years of internship are required. The purpose of internship is, of course, to learn how the theories, knowledge, and skills acquired in architectural school find their use and application in architects' services to the public. Therefore, you must work under the direction and control of an architect registered to practice in the state in which you are employed. You will receive a full and regular salary during this period from the architect who employs you. You are not obligated to stay in the same office for your entire internship.

In looking for that first job, you should consider firms of good reputation where you will be exposed to all phases of practice. This may mean a small to medium-size office or a larger firm for experience in projects involving large numbers of design, construction, and business management specialists. Your school's job placement office may assist you in contacting architects interested in current graduates, or you can simply write to firms of your own interest and knowledge, stating clearly and concisely your qualifications as you see them and the salary range you consider equitable. The architect will respond, suggesting an interview if your application fits the job description. Be punctual for your interview, and be prepared to illustrate the attitudes and aptitudes previously discussed in this chapter.

A portfolio presenting your studio projects and any experience you have accumulated will interest the architect. The intent of the interview is to engage you in conversation and try to understand how your skills and talents will contribute to the needs of the firm. In turn, you will try to confirm that the office will meet your educational needs.

While serving your internship, you will learn primarily through job assignments and observation and will gain experience from explanations and criticisms of your work. In most offices, there is no formal procedure or schedule for your internship work. Consequently, it is primarily your own responsibility to seek a wide range of learning experiences. You should avoid excessive specialization by seeking experience in the whole range of tasks performed in your employer's practice.

The National Council of Architectural Registration Boards and the American Institute of Architects have developed the Intern Development Program (IDP). The purpose of the IDP is to provide interns (and their employers) with a structured program encompassing a wide range of practical work tasks in preparation for examination and registration. IDP is available in all jurisdictions in the United States and will ultimately be offered by all architectural offices. In considering your first employment opportunity, you should inquire as to the availability of IDP in each interview situation. Results of IDP demonstrate quite clearly that the program benefits each intern fortunate enough to have participated in it.

The IDP publishes the *Emerging Professional's Companion* (EPC), which replaces the *AIA Supplementary Education Handbook*. The EPC is a free Web-based professional development resource that is designed to improve the quality of internship training. EPC activities challenge interns to develop the awareness, understanding, and skills needed to achieve the core competencies identified in each of the sixteen IDP training areas. The EPC is available at www.epcompanion.org. When first employed, you will be given simple assignments, such as to help complete presentation and working drawings. As your skill develops, you will be given responsibility to fully prepare working drawings for certain details or for selected portions of the project. Later, your work will include experience in all phases of design, as well as construction administration.

This comprehensive experience is not easily obtained in three short years of internship. You and your employer will need to work together to be sure you are exposed to the maximum range of office and project experiences. To ensure that you are benefiting from this maximum exposure, you are required to maintain a training record during your internship.

A full explanation of the Intern Development Program requirements can be obtained from the National Council of Architectural Registration Boards (NCARB). Visit www.ncarb.org for details.

Examination and Registration

Each of the fifty states, Guam, the Virgin Islands, the Northern Mariana Islands, Puerto Rico, and the District of Columbia have laws regulating the practice of architecture. There is some variation among these laws, but generally they prohibit the use of the title "architect" for those who are not licensed and make it unlawful to practice architecture without a license. Member board requirements are available at the NCARB website, www.ncarb.org/stateboards. It is imperative that you be familiar with the details of the legal requirements in your state.

The Architect Registration Examination (ARE) has been adopted for use by all fifty-five U.S. member boards and the Canadian provincial architectural associations. All divisions of the exam are administered exclusively on computers year-round at test centers throughout the United States, the U.S. territories, and Canada. Candidates may take the divisions in any order, and at any time and location they choose (subject to availability). Most test centers are open six days a week, fifty weeks a year.

The Architect Registration Examination

The Architect Registration Examination is developed by the National Council of Architectural Registration Boards and is composed of two sections covering the following nine divisions:

Multiple Choice Divisions
- Predesign (2.5 hours, 105 questions)
- General Structures (2.5 hours, 85 questions)
- Lateral Forces (2 hours, 75 questions)
- Mechanical and Electrical Systems (2 hours, 105 questions)
- Building Design/Materials and Methods (2 hours, 105 questions)
- Construction Documents and Services (3 hours, 115 questions)

Graphic Divisions (each division consists of two sections)
- Site Planning (1.5 hours, 2 vignettes; 1.5 hours, 3 vignettes)
- Building Planning (1 hour, 1 vignette; 4 hours, 1 vignette)
- Building Technology (2.5 hours, 3 vignettes; 2.75 hours, 3 vignettes)

The complete guidelines for the ARE are available at the NCARB website: www.ncarb.org/are/areguide.html.

Professional Practice and Continuing Education

Once you have passed the exam and earned your license to practice architecture, you may choose to work toward a partnership in an established firm or to establish your own firm by yourself or in partnership with one or more colleagues. You may choose to teach or do research for a large institution, or go into urban planning, building product sales and manufacturing, or one of many other salaried positions in public or private employment. The possibilities are almost unrestricted, and the direction you choose will probably become clear during your internship.

However, one important consideration underlies all these possibilities: do not put off earning your license to practice architecture! It is essential to your career.

Too many young people let the opportunity to become registered slip away from them after graduation by going directly into teaching, urban planning, or some other field that does not afford them the opportunity to fulfill the technical requirements of internship. Consequently, they are never eligible to take the registration examination. Later, they find that in their years away from school and practice, they have forgotten much of the technical knowledge required to pass the examination and that refresher courses just aren't sufficient to prepare them for some portions of it. Without the license, career potential is compromised.

Continuing progress in the techniques of environmental design and construction will present new challenges to you every day of your career, challenges to expand your knowledge, skills, and competence, and to guide younger associates along the path you already know so well. The AIA and other industry associations offer a multitude of professional development opportunities through conventions, symposia, research, publications, and participation in the work of local, state, and national association committees.

As an architect, the challenges and responsibilities are considerable and will be constantly demanding of your time and energies. But, as we have said before, you will be a professional to whom society looks as a guardian of its health, its safety, and its general welfare. For those who would answer these challenges, the demands could not be less.

Licensing and Reciprocity

As noted previously, the states and territories have licensing boards that regulate the practice of architecture within their respective jurisdictions. Since architects practice across state lines, all states and territories have reciprocal licensing agreements with other states and territories. The NCARB promotes uniform licensing procedures and otherwise furthers such reciprocity. There is no national law regulating the practice of architecture, nor a national license for such practice. However, the NCARB facilitates exchange of an architect's credentials through its programs to develop common licensing procedures.

To round out your view of the licensing requirements governing the practice of architecture, get the name and address of the registration board in your state and become familiar with the rules and regulations pertaining to the examination for and regulation of the practice of architecture. The name and address of the board can be obtained from the office of the city clerk in your hometown or the county clerk of your county. Or, you can visit http://ncarb.org/state boards/index.html to find the contact information for the registration board in your state. Individual board requirements are listed at the site. Licensing regulations of this sort may, at first reading, be difficult to understand. Your guidance counselor can be of assistance in pinpointing those parts of the regulations that will be of greatest interest to you at this point in your search for a career.

In addition to reciprocity among American states, an agreement has been reached between the NCARB and the Committee of Canadian Architectural Councils (CCAC) that provides for the reciprocal registration of architects who are practicing in a jurisdiction that has signed a Letter of Undertaking. This Letter of Undertaking provides for the acceptance of the conditions of the NCARB/CCAC Agreement and also permits the jurisdiction/province to stipulate any special requirements, such as demonstration of knowledge of local laws, seismic forces, personal interview, or other unique requirements that all applicants for registration must meet.

Architects with NCARB certification who are registered in and practice in a jurisdiction that has signed the Letter of Undertaking may transmit their NCARB Certificate Record to a jurisdiction/province that has also signed the Letter of Undertaking. Complete information about U.S./Canada reciprocity is available at http://ncarb.org/reciprocity/interrecognition.html.

7

THE ENVIRONMENTAL
DESIGN PROFESSIONS

TODAY THE CONSTRUCTION industry, with the leadership of the environmental design professions—architecture, engineering, landscape architecture, and urban planning—has the technical resources to enclose and control the climate of an entire urban area within a single structure. You know of large shopping malls, stadiums, and other big building complexes throughout North America that point to this possibility of completely enclosing and controlling a defined area of our physical environment. You also know of the rapid advancements being made in ground, water, and air transport facilities to service our physical environment. Further, you recognize the increasing attention being given to the remaking of existing urban areas and to the preservation and enhancement of our nation's natural resources—its open spaces, wilderness areas, water and air resources. All these activities involve the services of those trained and experienced in the environmental design professions. If we are to rebuild a good share of our existing development and preserve our remaining natural resources, it is easy to see that environmental designers have an immense task ahead of them. The career opportunities are commensurate with this great challenge.

Those directly involved in the design and construction of our environment are not the only members of the environmental design profession. As in every other vocation, the art and science of environmental design requires the services of those who teach its disciplines to others who search out and record and interpret its activities to society. Thus, these professions include many career opportunities for those whose basic training is in design but who wish to devote their talents to design education, archaeology, construction science, technical writing, or other fields that combine a background in design with a unique talent in a second discipline. Your future might well be in one of these combined careers.

Disciplines Within Environmental Design

To illustrate the broad range of career opportunities open to those who choose to enter the environmental design professions, we can make a simple checklist of some of the disciplines included in or related to these professions. In reviewing this list, you should note again that architecture is the basic art and science of the environmental design professions; that those trained in architecture therefore have the broadest choice of career opportunities in the design of our physical environment.

Primary Disciplines
Architecture
Engineering

Interior design
Landscape architecture
Planning

Component and Related Disciplines

Analysis	Economic and market potential
	Land use and feasibility
Programming	Functional relationships and space utilization
Promotion	Job development
	Real estate assembly
	Land and construction scheduling
Design	Area and space planning
	Urban design, transportation, utilities, and site planning
	Structural, mechanical, electrical, sanitary, acoustical, vibration, and similar engineering design
	Drafting, specification writing, product analysis
	Interior equipment planning
	Fine arts and graphics planning
Financing	Cost estimating and analysis
	Construction cost accounting
Construction	Bidding and contract negotiation
	Contract administration
	Construction management
	Maintenance and repair
Supporting	Archaeology and preservation
	Construction law

Insurance and sureties
Research and testing
Product development and
   fabrication
Education
Reporting and criticism
Photography, model making, and
   presentations
Computer applications
Information technology

Career Options

Those trained and experienced in architecture have a variety of career options available to them. You may choose to pursue one of these alternative careers after investing a few years in the profession and finding that a personal interest in one facet of the design and construction process has developed into an expertise recognized by others and requiring full-time attention to refine. Or, you may switch careers after having mastered the conventional practice of architecture. Here are five such alternative careers that have proved rewarding to the many architects who have chosen to pursue them.

Preservation and Rehabilitation

The study of the history of architecture is a basic interest of those drawn to the fields of architecture and other elements of environmental design. Courses in architectural history comprise a significant portion of the architect's education. For most architects, an interest in the roots of the art and science of architecture continues throughout their careers. In fact, this interest is one that architects share with the general public. For instance, a fair share of the recreation and tourism business is based upon a general popular fascination with our heritage and the lifestyles of our ancestors. If you were to vacation in Europe, for example, your itinerary would almost certainly focus on visiting structures and places important to the development of our Western culture. In this country, we have long given special recognition to places such as Mount Vernon and Monticello that are associated with our nation's early leaders.

In recent years, the growing popular interest in knowing more about and conserving our heritage has extended our concern for preserving more and more of our existing structures. Young families are interested in fixing up older homes, and businesses frequently look for opportunities to rehabilitate existing commercial structures. Public officials view the adaptive reuse of our older structures as an option equal to tearing down that structure and replacing it with a new facility. Federal, state, and local organizations devoted to preserving structures and districts have become important political forces in the establishment of public policy.

The movement in historic preservation and rehabilitation can take the form of saving entire blocks or districts as well as individual buildings. Further, the movement extends to all building types, from individual residences and commercial buildings to entire neighborhoods in urban areas. The interest may involve landmark structures of importance to our cultural heritage because of some person or event associated with that structure. It can also simply encompass a building or neighborhood having a special unity of design within a larger, mixed urban setting.

The saving and rehabilitation of these structures and districts has now become a significant career opportunity for architects. Rehabilitation work requires structural and other feasibility studies to determine the cost and time requirements of saving the structures and to find an adaptive use that may be placed in the rehabilitated facility. Most recently, changes in the tax legislation, building code requirements, and funding assistance have made investment in rehabilitation activities more attractive.

As a result of this growing interest in historic preservation, increasing numbers of public and private agencies and of architectural firms are pursuing these activities. Consequently, many students and practitioners are devoting portions of their careers to preservation. Given the recent renewed awareness of our cultural heritage and our concern for conservation of resources, it seems certain that preservation and rehabilitation services offered by the environmental design professions will continue to provide significant career opportunities.

Construction Management and Development

Construction management is a relatively new discipline within environmental design. It arises from the need to provide greater overall coordination to the design and construction processes from the beginning of programming through the completion of construction and the occupancy of the facility.

Construction management firms are frequently retained directly by an owner to advise and consult on the programming, design, and cost-estimating activities of the architect and to coordinate the work schedules, material deliveries, and trade jurisdiction of the various contractors. The objective of such services is to effect cost savings in the ways that elements of the building process are brought together and to reduce the length of time the project takes from conception to completion. Those who find their talents and interests taking them into construction techniques, cost-estimating procedures, and the business management aspects of construction find construction management an attractive career option. Building owners and investors find construction management services attractive because they provide professional counsel throughout the entire design/construction process. The owner and his or her financial partners can save considerable time in major building projects by using the construction management system.

City and Regional Planning

City planning and building is an ancient art. Among its earliest practitioners were the Romans who, in building military outposts to support their expanding empire, laid out a number of new cities with considerable precision. The sites of many of these new communities became, in later times, major European centers. European colonists, particularly the Spanish and, in some cases, the English, came to North America with well-developed ideas on how the various parts of a city should be laid out. Many South American capitals, for instance, display the influence of the initial city plans laid out by the church and military officials accompanying the early Spanish explorers. In our own country, Philadelphia, Washington, DC, and Savannah, Georgia, are examples of English and French influences on early city planning and building. During the Industrial Revolution, little attention was given to the art of building cities. Urban concentration extended across the landscape as a result of the real estate industry's skill at dividing up and selling off the land as rapidly as possible. The unrelieved grid patterns of many American cities west of the Alleghenies show this trend.

Interest in city planning revived in the late 1800s. A number of major American cities developed extensive plans for the remodeling and beautification of their central areas. Today, in cities such as Chicago, St. Louis, Denver, Cleveland, and San Francisco, this interest is evidenced in extensive parks, open space, and rather formal public buildings in their central areas. Much of this planning was the work of a small group of people frequently led by Daniel Burnham, a Chicago architect.

From the 1920s through the 1940s, growing interest in city and regional planning extended to increased zoning codes, subdivision regulations, and other controls placed upon the use and development of land. Following World War II, rapid population growth and increased use of automobiles resulted in a sudden need for more housing, schools, shopping centers, highways, industrial parks, airports, and other facilities. There was great concern that these facilities be adequately serviced by utilities and that they be properly related to one another. This concern gave rise to increasing interest in environmental pollution and conservation issues brought about by postwar construction.

Out of all this activity came the development and recognition of the city and regional planning profession with all its disciplines, ranging from resource planning and physical design, through urban sociology and economics, to political science and public management. Today, the planning profession offers varied and attractive career options to those trained and experienced in architecture. Many students who have completed their first degree in architecture choose to take advanced work in urban planning. Others find their first employment in public or private planning offices, which feature programs in urban design. The architect in private practice frequently contributes to city planning to some degree to better fit a building project into its neighborhood.

Given our increasing concern for the proper use of land-based resources, there can be little doubt that the planning profession will continue to offer many career opportunities to architects interested in urban design. These professions can be pursued in private practice or in public agencies. The architect/urban designer/city planner in the public agency will most likely find development of broad public policy to be the principal assignment. In private practice, this same person will find the principal work to be support of the public policy through the design and construction of a particular project. Thus, there is a choice between approaches to utilizing a wide range of talents and interests.

In the last several years, yet another unique combination of career opportunities has emerged and is being refined into a new discipline within the environmental design and construction field. One might refer to this new discipline as *city rebuilding*. Individuals and private firms who practice this discipline contract with municipalities to rebuild significant portions of the municipality. Work in and around the Baltimore Inner Harbor area is an example. Similar work has been completed in the Boston waterfront area, the Navy Pier facility in Chicago, and the South Street Seaport in Manhattan.

To date, these activities have concentrated on "people places," i.e., those areas of a city that have certain historic features that, if rehabilitated, promise to draw large numbers of visitors seeking relaxation and entertainment. They have brought a whole new level of ambience to the centers of those cities. These successes are producing private firms that specialize in the rehabilitation of the older parts of our cities. They bring a very high level of organizational talent, design sensitivity, and construction expertise to the client community, thereby relieving that community of the need for such on-staff talent. Their organizational talents include expertise in public and private financing and thorough knowledge of the many local, state, and federal regulations governing the design and construction of public facilities. These organizations are now turning their attention to the rehabilitation of the more commonplace retail, office, and industrial portions of our cities, and the opportunities for the architect, urban designer, and city planner are increasing.

Part of this growth in the city rebuilding field may be traced to our general recognition that our resources are limited and must be conserved. This suggests that our older cities should be rehabilitated as opposed to being abandoned in favor of new development on the edge of the city. Our renewed interest in our community's heritage is also part of the reason.

Communications

Communications are important in all human endeavors. In both the service industries and in the professions, where interpersonal relationships are basic to the provision of services to the buyer, communications are critical. In the environmental design professions, communications usually take the form of drawings or other fixed graphics and written text to cover those items not treated in the graphics. Thus the architect develops sketches, formal perspectives, working drawings, specifications, and various contract forms for communications with clients, contractors, subcontractors, and others essential to the design and construction process.

But an architect's communications do not begin or end with drawn and written materials. The architect must also develop verbal talents necessary for gaining approval of the designs developed in response to clients' needs. The architect's communications range across all available tools and techniques of exchanging information with those involved in the building process.

After some years of experience, an architect may find that he or she possesses a special talent—verbal, textual, or graphic—in the field of communications and will gain increasing recognition for those particular talents and abilities. In essence, that talent will be recognized as a particular ability to reduce a problem to its essentials, to organize the solution to that problem, and to clearly explain the solution to others. As this talent grows and is broadly recognized, the architect will be increasingly called upon as a communicator and will develop special techniques specially suited to her or his particular type of practice, audience, and personal sense of what tools he or she works best with: written, drawn, or spoken; print, graphic, film, or electronic media.

This increasing sophistication and growing expertise may well lead the architect into a full-time career in journalism, lecturing, teaching, film, television, graphic arts, or another facet of the communications industry.

This does not mean that the architect must necessarily leave the field of architecture to pursue this developing talent in communications. In larger environmental design offices, the architect may well find those talents devoted to the work of the firm: the promotion of services, the preparation of project reports, or the representation of the firm and the profession before the public. On the other hand, the architect with such skills may find career opportunities within the communications industries to be more attractive, and he or she may consider a switch of careers from architecture to communications.

Professional Associations

Professional and public interest associations are traditional American institutions. Chances are that you belong to one or more such groups. Examples might be a conservation society, local youth association, YMCA, YWCA, JCC, debate club, or similar group. Most likely you know adults who have long been members of a trade, professional, political, or specialized citizen group that expresses their interest in a particular subject on a local, state, or national level.

In the years since World War II, the number of nonprofit associations has grown immensely throughout the United States and Canada. This growth is the result of our increasing awareness of the need to take part in the shaping of public attitudes and subsequent programs affecting our working and living environments and our general quality of life. Many of these organizations offer attractive career opportunities for those trained in environmental design, and it is common for an architect, sometime during his or her career development, to be on the staff of such an organization.

A review of the Yellow Pages of a telephone directory in any major American city will reveal a considerable number of such associations. Washington, DC, of course, has thousands, since one of the principal purposes of such groups is to influence legislation. Similarly, most state capitals, or the major urban areas within each state, have a number of similar institutions.

While there are many large nationwide associations that can support a headquarters staff of several dozen professionals and technicians, there is a much larger number of local groups with several hundred members and a staff of only a few people. Typically, these groups depend upon membership dues, foundation grants, and special purpose study and research project funding for their financial bases. Their activities involve writing proposals for legislation, advocacy and lobbying before appropriate elected and appointed bodies, sponsorship of debate on public policy issues, public education programs, execution of research programs, and fund-raising to support all these varied activities.

The interests of these groups may range from the joining together of local professionals for the betterment of their own disciplines; to groups that sponsor improved local planning and housing programs; to regional and state organizations promoting the understanding of open space needs, historic preservation techniques, and similar environmental issues; and to national organizations of professional and citizen groups interested in environmental or other issues at the federal level. All these organizations require trained professional staff to execute programs responsive to the organization's interest. Obviously, a trained architect is often essential.

A staff job with one of these associations may be a part-time student position, a summer position, a graduate intern position, or a career as an association executive. Washington, DC, for instance, has many trained and experienced design professionals who have devoted the bulk of their careers to employment in professional associations. Salaries, benefits, and related work environments for the association executive are equivalent to those found in private firms and public agencies. A particular satisfaction of such a career is the contributions one can make linking public and private interest for the betterment of environmental design.

Schools of Architecture

THE LIST OF schools of architecture with programs accredited by the National Architectural Accrediting Board, Inc., is issued by the NAAB, 1735 New York Ave. NW, Washington, DC 20006. It includes all schools of architecture in the United States that offer programs leading to a professional degree acceptable to the profession and the law. NAAB also publishes a list of Canadian Schools of Architecture recognized by the Royal Architectural Institute of Canada. These lists are revised annually and are valid in detail only until the next lists are issued. The lists are available at the NAAB website, www.naab.org.

Schools of architecture within the United States include the institutions listed below. Not all of them offer accredited undergraduate degree programs. Some are exclusively graduate schools.

Alabama

Auburn University
College of Architecture, Design, & Construction
202 Dudley Commons
Auburn, AL 36849
(B.Arch.)
www.arch.auburn.edu

Tuskegee University
Department of Architecture
Tuskegee Institute, AL 36088
(B.Arch)
www.tuskegee.edu/global/category.asp?C=35304

Arizona

Arizona State University
School of Architecture & Landscape Architecture
P.O. Box 871605
Tempe, AZ 85287-1605
(M.Arch.)
www.asu.edu/caed/sala

Frank Lloyd Wright School of Architecture
FLLWSA Taliesin West
12621 N. Frank Lloyd Wright Blvd.
Scottsdale, AZ 85261-4430
(M.Arch)
www.taliesin.edu
October 15 to May 15
(May 16 to October 14, see Wisconsin entry)

University of Arizona
Department of Architecture
Tempe, AZ 85721
(B.Arch)
www.architecture.arizona.edu

Arkansas

University of Arkansas
School of Architecture
120 Vol Walker Hall
Fayetteville, AR 72701
(B.Arch)
www.uark.edu/~archsite

California

Academy of Art University
School of Architecture
P.O. Box 193844
San Francisco, CA 94119-3844
(M.Arch)
www.academyart.edu/arh

California College of the Arts
School of Architectural Studies
1111 Eighth St.
San Francisco, CA 94107-2247
(B.Arch, M.Arch)
www.cca.edu/academics/barch

California Polytechnic State University
College of Architecture and Environmental Design
San Luis Obispo, CA 93407
(B.Arch)
www.arch.calpoly.edu

California State Polytechnic University–Pomona
Department of Architecture
3801 W. Temple Ave.
Pomona, CA 91768
(B.Arch, M.Arch)
www.csupomona.edu/~arc

NewSchool of Architecture & Design
Architecture College
1249 F St.
San Diego, CA 92101
(B.Arch, M.Arch)
www.newschoolarch.edu

Southern California Institute of Architecture
960 E. Third St.
Los Angeles, CA 90013
(B.Arch, M.Arch)
www.sciarc.edu

University of California at Berkeley
Department of Architecture
232 Wurster Hall, MC #1800
Berkeley, CA 94720-1800
(M.Arch)
www.ced.berkeley.edu

University of California at Los Angeles
Department of Architecture and Urban Design
Box 951467
Los Angeles, CA 90095-1467
(M.Arch)
www.aud.ucla.edu

University of Southern California
School of Architecture
Watt Hall, Ste. 204
Los Angeles, CA 90089-0291
(B.Arch, M.Arch)
www.usc.edu/dept/architecture

Woodbury University
School of Architecture & Design
1060 8th Ave., Ste. 200
San Diego, CA 92101
(B.Arch)
www.woodbury.edu/nav3left.aspx?pgid=1032

Colorado

University of Colorado at Boulder
College of Architecture & Planning
Boulder, CO 80309
(M.Arch)
www.cudenver.edu/academics/colleges/architectureplanning/
    default.htm

University of Colorado at Denver
College of Architecture & Planning
1250 14th St., Annex
Campus Box 167
P.O. Box 173364
Denver, CO 80217-3364
(M.Arch)
www.cudenver.edu/academics/colleges/architecture
    planning/default.htm

Connecticut

University of Hartford
Department of Architecture
200 Bloomfield Ave.
West Hartford, CT 06117
(Candidate for M.Arch)
http://uhaweb.hartford.edu/ceta

Yale University
Department of Architecture
New Haven, CT 06520
(M.Arch)
www.architecture.yale.edu

District of Columbia

Catholic University of America
School of Architecture and Planning
620 Michigan Ave. NE
Washington, DC 20064
(M.Arch)
http://architecture.cua.edu

Howard University
School of Architecture and Design
2300 Sixth St. NW
Washington, DC 20059
(B.Arch)
www.howard.edu/ceacs

Florida

Florida A&M University
School of Architecture
1936 S. MLK Blvd.
Tallahassee, FL 32307
(B.Arch, M.Arch)
www.famusoa.net

Florida Atlantic University
School of Architecture
FAU/BCC Higher Education Complex
111 E. Las Olas Blvd.
Fort Lauderdale, FL 33301
(B.Arch)
www.fau.edu/divdept/caupa/arch/index.html

Florida International University
School of Architecture
University Park Campus
11200 SW 8th St.
Paul L. Cejas Architecture Bldg.
PCA 272
Miami, FL 33199
(M.Arch)
www.fiu.edu/~soa

University of Florida
School of Architecture
College of Design, Construction, and Planning
331 ARC
P.O. Box 115701
Gainesville, FL 32611-5701
(M.Arch)
www.dcp.ufl.edu

University of Miami
School of Architecture
1223 Dickinson Dr.
Coral Gables, FL 33146
(B.Arch, M.Arch)
www.arc.miami.edu

University of South Florida
School of Architecture and Community Design
3702 Spectrum Blvd., #180
Tampa, FL 33612
(M.Arch)
www.arch.usf.edu

Georgia

Georgia Institute of Technology
College of Architecture
Atlanta, GA 30322
(M.Arch)
www.coa.gatech.edu

Savannah College of Art and Design
P.O. Box 3146
Savannah, GA 31402-3146
(M.Arch)
www.scad.edu/academic/majors/arch/index.cfm

Southern Polytechnic State University
Department of Architecture
1100 S. Marietta Pkwy.
Marietta, GA 30060
(B.Arch)
www.spsu.edu/home/academics/architecture.html

Hawaii

University of Hawaii at Manoa
School of Architecture
2500 Campus Rd.
Hawaii Hall 202
Honolulu, HI 96822
(D.Arch)
http://web1.arch.hawaii.edu

Idaho

University of Idaho
Architecture Department
AAS 207
University of Idaho
Moscow, ID 83844-2451
(M.Arch)
www.class.uidaho.edu/arch

Illinois

Illinois Institute of Technology
Department of Architecture
3300 S. Federal St.
Chicago, IL 60616-3793
(B.Arch, M.Arch)
www.iit.edu/colleges/arch

Judson College
Department of Architecture
1151 N. State St.
Elgin, IL 60123-1498
(M.Arch)
www.judson-il.edu/grad/index.aspx?id=184

University of Illinois at Chicago
School of Architecture
Jefferson Hall
929 W. Harrison St.
Chicago, IL 60607
(M.Arch)
www.arch.uic.edu

University of Illinois at Urbana–Champaign
School of Architecture
117 Temple Hoyne Buell Hall
611 Lorado Taft Dr., MC-621
Champaign, IL 61820
(M.Arch)
www.arch.uiuc.edu

Indiana

Ball State University
College of Architecture and Planning
AB 104
Muncie, IN 47306
(B.Arch.)
www.bsu.edu/cap

University of Notre Dame
School of Architecture
110 Bond Hall
Notre Dame, IN 46556
(B.Arch, M.Arch)
http://architecture.nd.edu

Iowa

Iowa State University
Department of Architecture
Ames, IA 50011
(B.Arch, M.Arch)
www.arch.iastate.edu

Kansas

Kansas State University
College of Architecture, Planning, and Design
211 Seton Hall
Manhattan, KS 66506
(B.Arch)
www.capd.ksu.edu

University of Kansas
School of Architecture and Urban Design
1465 Jayhawk Blvd.
205 Marvin Hall
Lawrence, KS 66045-7614
(B.Arch, M.Arch)
www.saud.ku.edu

Kentucky

University of Kentucky
School of Architecture
College of Design
117 Pence Hall
Lexington, KY 40506-0041
(B.Arch)
www.uky.edu/design/architecture.htm

Louisiana

Louisiana State University
School of Architecture
136 Atkinson Hall
Baton Rouge, LA 70803-5710
(B.Arch, M.Arch)
www.arch.lsu.edu

Louisiana Tech University
School of Architecture
Box 3147
Ruston, LA 71270
(B.Arch)
www.latech.edu/tech/liberal-arts/architecture

Southern University and A&M College
School of Architecture
Baton Rouge, LA 70813
(B.Arch)
www.susa.subr.edu

Tulane University
Department of Architecture
New Orleans, LA 70118
(B.Arch, M.Arch)
www.tulane.edu

University of Louisiana at Lafayette
School of Architecture and Design
P.O. Box 43850
Lafayette, LA 70504-0001
(B.Arch, M.Arch)
http://soad.louisiana.edu

Maryland

Morgan State University
Institute of Architecture and Planning
2201 Argonne Dr.
Montebello B107
Baltimore, MD 21251
(M.Arch)
www.morgan.edu/academics/iap/index.html

University of Maryland
School of Architecture, Planning, and Preservation
College Park, MD 20742
(M.Arch)
www.arch.umd.edu

Massachusetts

Boston Architectural Center
320 Newbury St.
Boston, MA 02115
(B.Arch, M.Arch)
www.the-bac.edu

Harvard University
Department of Architecture
School of Design
48 Quincy St.
Cambridge, MA 02138
(M.Arch)
www.gsd.harvard.edu

Massachusetts Institute of Technology
Department of Architecture
77 Massachusetts Ave.
Room 7-337
Cambridge, MA 02139-2307
(M.Arch)
www.architecture.mit.edu

Northeastern University
Department of Architecture
151 Ryder Hall
Boston, MA 02115
(M.Arch)
www.architecture.neu.edu

Wentworth Institute of Technology
Department of Architecture
550 Huntington Ave.
Boston, MA 02115-5998
(B.Arch)
www.wit.edu/prospective/academics/barc.html

Michigan

Andrews University
Division of Architecture
Berrien Springs, MI 49104
(B.Arch, M.Arch)
www.arch.andrews.edu

Lawrence Technological University
College of Architecture and Design
21000 W. Ten Mile Rd.
Southfield, MI 48075-1058
(M.Arch)
http://www.ltu.edu/architecture_and_design

University of Detroit Mercy
School of Architecture
4001 W. McNichols Rd.
Detroit, MI 48221
(B.Arch, M.Arch)
http://architecture.udmercy.edu

University of Michigan
Taubman College of Architecture and Urban Planning
2000 Bonisteel Blvd., Rm. 2150
Ann Arbor, MI 48109-2069
(M.Arch)
www.tcaup.umich.edu

Mississippi

Mississippi State University
Department of Architecture
College of Architecture, Art, and Design
Mississippi State, MS 39762
(B.Arch)
www.msstate.edu

Missouri

Drury University
Hammons School of Architecture
900 N. Benton Ave.
Springfield, MO 65802
(B.Arch)
http://www.drury.edu/section/section.cfm?sid=48

Washington University in St. Louis
School of Architecture
Campus Box 1079
One Brookings Dr.
St. Louis, MO 63130
(M.Arch)
www.arch.wustl.edu

Minnesota

University of Minnesota Twin Cities
Department of Architecture
College of Architecture and Landscape Architecture
145 Rapson Hall
89 Church St. SE
Minneapolis, MN 55455
(M.Arch)
www.cala.umn.edu

Montana

Montana State University–Bozeman
School of Architecture
Cheever Hall
Bozeman, MT 59717
(M.Arch)
www.arch.montana.edu

Nebraska

University of Nebraska–Lincoln
College of Architecture
Lincoln, NE 68588
(M.Arch)
http://archweb.unl.edu

Nevada

University of Nevada–Las Vegas
School of Architecture
4505 Maryland Pkwy.
Box 454018
Las Vegas, NV 89154
(M.Arch)
http://architecture.unlv.edu

New Jersey

New Jersey Institute of Technology
New Jersey School of Architecture
University Heights
Newark, NJ 07102-1982
(B.Arch, M.Arch)
http://architecture.njit.edu

Princeton University
School of Architecture
Princeton, NJ 08554-t5264
(M.Arch)
www.princeton.edu/~soa

New Mexico

University of New Mexico
School of Architecture and Planning
Albuquerque, NM 87131
(M.Arch)
www.cala.unm.edu/architecture

New York

City College of New York
School of Architecture
Convent Ave. at 138th St.
New York, NY 10031
(B.Arch)
www.ccny.cuny.edu/architecture/archprog/intropage.htm

Columbia University
Graduate School of Architecture, Planning, and Preservation
Avery Hall
New York, NY 10027
(M.Arch)
www.arch.columbia.edu

The Cooper Union
Chanin School of Architecture
30 Cooper Sq.
New York, NY 10003
(B.Arch)
www.cooper.edu/architecture

Cornell University
Department of Architecture
College of Architecture, Art, and Planning
129 Sibley Dome
Ithaca, NY 14853
(B.Arch, M.Arch)
www.aap.cornell.edu

New York Institute of Technology
School of Architecture and Design
1855 Broadway
New York, NY 10023-7692
(B.Arch)
www.nyit.edu/architecture

Parsons School of Design/New School University
Department of Architecture
55 Fifth Ave.
New York, NY 10017
(M.Arch)
www.parsons.edu/architecture

Pratt Institute
School of Architecture
Higgins Hall, First Fl.
200 Willoughby Ave.
Brooklyn, NY 11205
(B.Arch, M.Arch)
www.pratt.edu/arch

Rensselaer Polytechnic Institute
School of Architecture
110 Eighth St.
Troy, NY 12180
(B.Arch, M.Arch)
www.arch.rpi.edu

Syracuse University
School of Architecture
103 Slocum Hall
Syracuse, NY 13244-1250
(B.Arch, M.Arch)
http://soa.syr.edu

University at Buffalo
School of Architecture and Planning
112 Hayes Hall
3435 Main St.
Buffalo, NY 14214-3087
(M.Arch)
www.ap.buffalo.edu

North Carolina

North Carolina State University
Department of Architecture
College of Design
Campus Box 7701
Raleigh, NC 27695
(B.Arch, M.Arch)
http://ncsudesign.org/content

University of North Carolina at Charlotte
College of Architecture
9201 University City Blvd.
Storrs Hall
Charlotte, NC 28223-0001
(B.Arch, M.Arch)
www.coa.uncc.edu

North Dakota

North Dakota State University
Department of Architecture and Landscape Architecture
P.O. Box 5285, SU Station
Fargo, ND 58105
(B.Arch)
www.ndsu.edu/arch

Ohio

Kent State University
College of Architecture and Environmental Design
200 Taylor Hall
Kent, OH 44242-0001
(B.Arch, M.Arch)
www.caed.kent.edu

Miami University
Department of Architecture and Interior Design
101 Alumni Hall
Oxford, OH 45056
(M.Arch)
http://fnaxbox1.fna.muohio.edu/arcweb/index2/index.html

Ohio State University
Department of Architecture
Knowlton School of Architecture
275 W. Woodruff Ave.
Columbus, OH 43210-1138
(M.Arch)
http://knowlton.osu.edu

University of Cincinnati
College of Design, Architecture, Art, and Planning
P.O. Box 210016
Cincinnati, OH 45221-0016
(B.Arch, M.Arch)
www.daap.uc.edu

Oklahoma

Oklahoma State University
School of Architecture
College of Engineering, Architecture, and Technology
101 Architecture Bldg.
Stillwater, OK 74078
(B.Arch)
www.ceat.okstate.edu

University of Oklahoma
College of Architecture
830 Van Vleet Oval
Norman, OK 73019
(B.Arch, M.Arch)
www.ou.edu/architecture

Oregon

University of Oregon
School of Architecture and Allied Arts
105 Lawrence Hall
Eugene, OR 97403
(B.Arch, M.Arch)
http://aaa.uoregon.edu

Pennsylvania

Carnegie Mellon University
School of Architecture
201 College of Fine Arts
Pittsburgh, PA 15213
(B.Arch)
www.arc.cmu.edu

Drexel University
Department of Architecture
College of Media Arts and Design
3141 Chestnut St.
Philadelphia, PA 19104
(B.Arch)
www.drexel.edu/academics/comad

Pennsylvania State University
Department of Architecture
College of Arts and Architecture
111 Arts Bldg.
University Park, PA 16802
(B.Arch)
www.artsandarchitecture.psu.edu

Philadelphia University
School of Architecture
School House La. & Henry Ave.
Philadelphia, PA 19144-5497
(B.Arch)
www.philau.edu/schools/add/index.htm

Temple University
Architecture Program
Tyler School of Art
1947 N. 12th St.
Philadelphia, PA 19122
(B.Arch)
www.temple.edu/tyler

University of Pennsylvania
Department of Architecture
207 Meyerson Hall
Philadelphia, PA 19104-6311
(B.Arch)
www.design.upenn.edu/new/arch/index.php

Puerto Rico

Polytechnic University of Puerto Rico
New School of Architecture
P.O. Box 192017
San Juan, PR 00919-2017
(B.Arch)
www.pupr.edu/arqpoli/homepage.htm

Universidad de Puerto Rico
Department of Architecture
P.O. Box 23336
San Juan, PR 00931-3336
(M.Arch)
www.upr.edu

Rhode Island

Rhode Island School of Design
Architecture Department
Two College St.
Providence, RI 02903-2784
(B.Arch, M.Arch)
www.risd.edu

Roger Williams University
School of Architecture, Art, and Historic Preservation
One Old Ferry Rd.
Bristol, RI 02809
(B.Arch, M.Arch)
http://arch.rwu.edu/saahp_content.html

South Carolina

Clemson University
School of Architecture
145 Lee Hall
Clemson, SC 29634
(M.Arch)
www.clemson.edu/caah/architecture

Tennessee

University of Tennessee–Knoxville
College of Architecture and Design
1715 Volunteer Blvd.
Knoxville, TN 37996-2400
(B.Arch, M.Arch)
www.arch.utk.edu

Texas

Prairie View A&M University
School of Architecture
P.O. Box 519
Prairie View, TX 77446-0519
(B.Arch, M.Arch)
www.pvamu.edu/content/architect

Rice University
Rice School of Architecture
MS-50
6100 Main St.
Houston, TX 77005
(B.Arch, M.Arch)
www.arch.rice.edu

Texas A&M University
College of Architecture
College Station, TX 77843-3137
(M.Arch)
http://archweb.tamu.edu/architecture

Texas Tech University
College of Architecture
Lubbock, TX 79409
(M.Arch)
www.ttu.edu/colleges/arch.php

University of Houston
College of Architecture
4800 Calhoun Rd.
Houston, TX 77204
(B.Arch, M.Arch)
www.uh.edu/academics/catalog/arc

University of Texas–Arlington
School of Architecture
Box 19108
601 Nedderman Dr.
Arlington, TX 76019-0108
(M.Arch)
www.uta.edu/architecture

University of Texas–Austin
School of Architecture
One University Station, B7500
Austin, TX 78712-0222
(B.Arch, M.Arch)
www.utexas.edu/dept/#architecture

University of Texas–San Antonio
College of Architecture
501 W. Durango Blvd.
San Antonio, TX 78207
(M.Arch)
www.utsa.edu/architecture

Utah

University of Utah
College of Architecture and Planning
201 S. Presidents Circle
Salt Lake City, UT 84112
(M.Arch)
www.arch.utah.edu

Virginia

Hampton University
Department of Architecture
School of Engineering and Technology
Hampton, VA 23668
(B.Arch, M.Arch)
www.hamptonu.edu/academics/schools/engineering/architecture

University of Virginia
School of Architecture
Campbell Hall
P.O. Box 400122
Charlottesville, VA 22904-4122
(M.Arch)
www.arch.virginia.edu

Virginia Polytechnic Institute and State University
Department of Architecture
College of Architecture and Urban Studies
201 Cowgill Hall
Virginia Tech (0205)
Blacksburg, VA 24061
(B.Arch, M.Arch)
www.arch.vt.edu

Washington

University of Washington
Department of Architecture
College of Architecture and Urban Planning
Box 355720
Seattle, WA 98195-5720
(M.Arch)
www.caup.washington.edu

Washington State University
School of Architecture and Construction Management
College of Engineering and Architecture
P.O. Box 642220
Pullman, WA 99164-2220
(B.Arch, M.Arch)
http://academics.wsu.edu/fields/study.asp?id=arch

Wisconsin

Frank Lloyd Wright School of Architecture
FLLWSA Taliesin
5481 County Hwy. C
Spring Green, WI 53588
(M.Arch)
www.taliesin.edu
May 16 to October 14
(October 15 to May 15, see Arizona entry)

University of Wisconsin–Milwaukee
Department of Architecture
School of Architecture and Urban Planning
P.O. Box 413
Milwaukee, WI 53201-0413
(M.Arch)
www.uwm.edu/sarup

Accredited Programs in Canada

The following list includes programs in Canadian universities that are accredited by the Canadian Architectural Certification Board.

Carleton University
School of Architecture
202 Architecture Bldg.
1125 Colonel By Dr.
Ottawa, ON K1S 5B6
(M.Arch)
www.arch.carleton.ca

Dalhousie University
School of Architecture
P.O. Box 1000
Halifax, NS B3J 2X4
(M.Arch)
http://architectureandplanning.dal.ca

McGill University
School of Architecture
Macdonald-Harrington Bldg.
815 Sherbrooke St. West
Montreal, QC H3A 2K6
(B.Arch, M.Arch)
www.mcgill.ca/architecture

Université Laval
École d'architecture
Faculté d'aménagement, d'architecture et des arts visuels
Édifice du Vieux-Séminaire de Québec
1, côte de la Fabrique
Québec, QC G1R 3V6
(M.Arch)
www.ulaval.ca/sg/annuaires/fac/aam.html

Université de Montreal
École d'architecture
Pavillon de la Faculté de l'aménagement
Local 2076–Secrétariat
2940, chemin de la Côte-Ste-Catherine
Montréal, QC H3T 1B9
(M.Arch)
www.arc.umontreal.ca

University of British Columbia
School of Architecture
6333 Memorial Blvd., Rm. 402
Vancouver, BC V6T 1Z2
(M.Arch)
www.arch.ubc.ca

University of Calgary
Faculty of Environmental Design
2500 University Dr. NW
Calgary, AB T2N 1N4
(M.Arch)
www.evds.ucalgary.ca

University of Manitoba
Faculty of Architecture
201 Russell Bldg.
Winnipeg, MB R3T 2N2
(M.Arch)
www.umanitoba.ca/faculties/architecture

University of Toronto
Faculty of Architecture, Landscape, and Design
230 College St.
Toronto, ON M5T 1R2
(B.Arch, M.Arch)
www.ald.utoronto.ca

University of Waterloo
School of Architecture
Faculty of Engineering
7 Melville St. South
Cambridge ON N1S 2H4
(M.Arch)
www.architecture.uwaterloo.ca

In addition to these schools that either offer programs accredited by NAAB or that are recognized by the Royal Institute, there are a number of other schools in the United States and Canada that offer some programs in architecture. All are members of the Association of Collegiate Schools of Architecture (ACSA). ACSA publishes the *Guide to Architecture Schools*, 7th edition. The book provides information on more than two hundred schools, as well as convenient demographic information and statistics. Visit www.acsa-arch.org for ordering information.

After reviewing a selection of the materials indicated above, you should then review the catalogs and other materials from schools of interest, consult with your guidance counselor, and secure his or her help in analyzing this information. Your objective should be the selection of those schools most nearly matching your qualifications and interests. Your counselor can be of real assistance in analyzing the details presented in the information you have gathered at this stage.

General Education Information

A most convenient general reference for all information relating to architectural education is the Director, Education Programs, The American Institute of Architects, 1735 New York Avenue NW, Washington, DC 20006-5292. Visit its website (www.aia.org/ed _arched) for general information on any aspect of architectural education, financial aid, internship and licensing, and career and professional concerns. The site also includes links to other organizations providing detailed information on these concerns.

APPENDIX B

Professional Associations

THE NAMES AND addresses of the principal professional and trade associations that represent the different architectural vocations are listed here. You may wish to contact them for additional information on careers in their particular fields.

Design Group

Architects

The American Institute of Architects (AIA)
1735 New York Ave. NW
Washington, DC 20006
www.aia.org

Royal Architecture Institute of Canada (RAIC)
330-55 rue Murray St.
Ottawa, ON K1N 5M3
www.raic.org

Interior Designers

American Society of Interior Designers (ASID)
600 Massachusetts Ave. NE
Washington, DC 20002-6006
www.asid.org

Interior Designers of Canada (IDC)
260 King St. East, Ste. 414
Toronto, ON M5A 1K3
www.interiordesigncanada.org

Urban Planners

American Planning Association (APA)
1776 Massachusetts Ave. NW
Washington, DC 20036-1904
www.planning.org

Canadian Institute of Planners (CIP)
116 Albert St., Ste. 801
Ottawa, ON K1P 5G3
www.cip-icu.ca

Canadian Society for Civil Engineering (CSCE)
4920 de Maisonneuve Blvd. West, Ste. 201
Montreal, QC H3Z 1N1
www.csce.ca

Civil Engineers
American Society of Civil Engineers (ASCE)
1801 Alexander Bell Dr.
Reston, VA 20191
www.asce.org

HVAC Engineers

American Society of Heating, Refrigerating, & Air-Conditioning
Engineers (ASHRAE)
P.O. Box 95812
Atlanta, GA 30347
www.ashrae.org

Heating, Refrigeration, and Air Conditioning Institute of
Canada (HRAI)
5045 Orbitor Dr.
Bldg. 11, Ste. 300
Mississauga, ON LW4 4Y4
www.hrai.ca

Mechanical Engineers

American Society of Mechanical Engineers (ASME)
Three Park Ave.
New York, NY 10016-5990
www.asme.org

Canadian Society for Mechanical Engineering (CSME)
P.O. Box 23027, Westgate Postal Outlet
Cambridge, ON N1S 4Z6
www.csme-scgm.ca

Landscape Architects

American Society of Landscape Architects (ASLA)
636 Eye St. NW
Washington, DC 20001-3786
www.asla.org

Canadian Society of Landscape Architects (CSLA)
P.O. Box 13594
Ottawa, ON K2K 1X6
www.csla.ca

Consulting Engineers

American Council of Engineering Companies (ACEC)
1015 15th St. NW, 8th Fl.
Washington, DC 20005-2605
www.acec.org

Electrical Engineers

Institute of Electrical & Electronics Engineers (IEEE)
1828 L St. NW, Ste. 1202
Washington, DC 20036-5104
www.ieee.org

Lighting Engineers

Illuminating Engineering Society of North America (IESNA)
120 Wall St., 17th Fl.
New York, NY 10005
www.iesna.org

Engineers

American Association of Engineering Societies (AAES)
1828 L St. NW
Washington, DC 20036
www.aaes.org

Canadian Council of Professional Engineers
180 Elgin St., Ste. 1100
Ottawa, ON K2P 2K3
www.ccpe.ca

Engineering Institute of Canada
1295 Hwy. 2 E
Kingston ON K7L 4V1
www.eic-ici.ca

National Society of Professional Engineers (NSPE)
1420 King St.
Alexandria, VA 22314
www.nspe.org

When contacting the design group organizations listed above, you should indicate that you want information on career opportunities in their segment of the construction industry. As you can imagine, some of the organizations represent professionals in other industries as well as construction. For instance, the membership of the last organization listed, NSPE, includes engineers from many different kinds of industries and in both public and private employ.

Constructor Group

General Construction Contracting

Associated Builders and Contractors (ABC)
4250 N. Fairfax Dr., 9th Fl.
Arlington, VA 22203-1607
www.abc.org

Associated General Contractors of America, Inc. (AGC)
333 John Carlyle St., Ste. 200
Alexandria, VA 22314
www.agc.org

Canadian Construction Association (CCA)
75 Albert St., Ste. 400
Ottawa, ON K1P 5E7
www.cca-acc.com

Building Trades

Building & Construction Trades Department
AFL-CIO
815 16th St., Ste. 600
Washington, DC 20006
www.buildingtrades.org

Construction Specification

Construction Specifications Canada (CSC)
120 Carlton St., Ste. 312
Toronto, ON M5A 4K2
www.csc-dcc.ca

Construction Specifications Institute (CSI)
99 Canal Center Plaza, Ste. 300
Alexandria, VA 22314
www.csinet.org

Building Systems Contracting

Associated Specialty Contractors
3 Bethesda Metro Center, Ste. 1100
Bethesda, MD 20814
www.assoc-spec-con.org

Home Building Contracting

Canadian Home Builders' Association (CHBA)
www.chba.ca

National Association of Home Builders (NAHB)
1201 15th St. NW
Washington, DC 20005
www.nahb.org

Support Group

Construction Financing

American Bankers Association
1120 Connecticut Ave. NW
Washington, DC 20036
www.aba.com

Canadian Bankers Association
Box 348
Commerce Court West
199 Bay St., 30th Fl.
Toronto, ON M5L 1G2
www.cba.ca

Construction Law

American Bar Association
321 N. Clark St.
Chicago, IL 60610
www.abanet.org

Canadian Bar Association
500-865 Carling Ave.
Ottawa, ON K1S 5S8
www.cba.org

Land and Building Appraisals

Appraisal Institute
550 W. Van Buren St., Ste. 1000
Chicago, IL 60607
www.appraisalinstitute.org

Insuring Construction and Building

American Insurance Association
1130 Connecticut Ave. NW, Ste. 1000
Washington, DC 20036
www.aiadc.org

Insurance Bureau of Canada (IBC)
151 Yonge St., Ste. 1900
Toronto, ON M5C 2W7
www.ibc.ca

Building Code Writing and Administration

International Code Council (ICC)
5203 Leesburg Pike, Ste. 600
Falls Church, VA 22041
www.iccsafe.org

All Elements of the Construction Industry

Canadian Chamber of Commerce
Delta Office Tower
350 Sparks St., Ste. 501
Ottawa, ON K1R 7S8
www.chamber.ca

Chamber of Commerce of the United States
1615 H St. NW
Washington, DC 20062-2000
www.uschamber.com

Real Estate

Canadian Real Estate Association (CREA)
344 Slater St., Ste. 1600
Ottawa, ON K1R 7Y3
www.crea.ca

National Association of Realtors (NAR)
430 N. Michigan Ave.
Chicago, IL 60611-4087
www.realtor.org

Facility Management

International Facility Management Association (IFMA)
1 E. Greenway Plaza, Ste. 1100
Houston, TX 77046-0194
www.ifma.org

Federal Government Careers in Design & Construction

Office of Personnel Management (OPM)
1900 E St. NW
Washington, DC 20415-1000
www.opm.gov

Community Development

Urban Land Institute (ULI)
1025 Thomas Jefferson St. NW, Ste. 500 West
Washington, DC 20007
www.uli.org

Construction Financing

America's Community Bankers
900 19th St. NW, Ste. 400
Washington, DC 20006
www.acbankers.org

When contacting any of the organizations listed above, you should indicate that you want information on career opportunities in the segment of the construction industry they represent. As you can imagine, some of these organizations have many interests outside the construction industry.

APPENDIX C

Related Reading

THERE ARE THOUSANDS of books available on the subject of architecture. Many of them go into great detail on special subjects within the general field, such as the history of architecture, various aspects of office practice, or famous modern architects. Here we list several references that, if taken together, will give you a comprehensive overview of the art, science, and practice of architecture.

Allen, Edward, and Joseph Iano. *Fundamentals of Building Construction: Materials and Methods*, 4th edition. New York: Wiley, 2003.

Colquhoun, Alan. *Modern Architecture*. Oxford: Oxford University Press, 2002.

Demkin, Joseph A. *The Architect's Handbook of Professional Practice*. Washington, DC: The American Institute of Architects, 2004.

Giedion, Sigfried. *Space, Time, and Architecture: The Growth of a New Tradition*, 5th revised and enlarged edition. Cambridge, Mass.: The Harvard University Press, 2003.

Harris, Michael. *Professional Architectural Photography*, 3rd edition. Burlington, Mass.: Elsevier Inc., 2001.

Hearn, Fil. *Ideas That Shaped Buildings*. Cambridge, Mass.: MIT Press, 2003.

Iloniemi, Laura. *Is It All About Image: How PR Works in Architecture* (Architecture in Practice). New York: Academy Press, 2004.

Jefferis, Alan, and David Madsen. *Architectural Drafting and Design*, 4th edition. Clifton Park, N.Y.: Thomson Delmar, 2000.

Kostof, Spiro. *The City Assembled: The Elements of Urban Form Through History*. London: Thames & Hudson, 2005.

Kostof, Spiro. *The Architect*. Oxford: Oxford University Press, 1989.

Merritt, Frederick S., and Jonathan T. Ricketts. *Building Design and Construction Handbook*, 6th edition. New York: McGraw-Hill, 2000.

Murphy, Michael D. *Landscape Architecture Theory: An Evolving Body of Thought*. Long Grove, Ill.: Waveland Press, 2005.

Piotrowski, Christine. *Professional Practice for Interior Designers*, 3rd edition. New York: Wiley, 2001.

Stasiowski, Frank A. *Staying Small Successfully: A Guide for Architects, Engineers, and Design Professionals*, 2nd edition. New York: Wiley, 2001.

Stipe, Margo. *Frank Lloyd Wright: The Interactive Portfolio*. Philadelphia: Running Press Book Publishers, 2004.

Strom, Steven, Kurt Nathan, Jake Woland, and David Lamm. *Site Engineering for Landscape Architects*, 4th edition. New York: Wiley, 2004.

Toy, Maggie (editor). *The Architect: Women in Contemporary Architecture*. New York: Watson-Guptill Publications, 2001.

Wakita, Osamu A., and Richard M. Linde. *The Professional Practice of Architectural Working Drawings*, 3rd edition. New York: Wiley, 2000.

Wasserman, Barry, Patrick J. Sullivan, and Gregory Palermo. *Ethics and the Practice of Architecture*. New York: Wiley, 2000.

Wright, Frank Lloyd. *An Autobiography*. Petaluma, Calif.: Pomegranate Communications, 2005.

About the Author

Robert J. Piper, a native of Byron, Illinois, earned his undergraduate degree in architectural engineering at the University of Illinois and graduate degree in city and regional planning at Cornell University. After working as a licensed architect, he was appointed to the post of Director of Professional Services for the American Institute of Architects (AIA) in Washington, DC, where he edited the *AIA Documents* and the *AIA Architects Handbook of Professional Practice*. Piper then became deputy director for the Northeastern Illinois Planning Commission, the public regional planning agency serving the six-county Chicago metropolitan area.

Piper also served as Director of Community Development for the City of Highland Park, Illinois, coordinating design and construction of the city's central business district redevelopment project. He retired in 1991 and continues to serve the environmental design professions as a volunteer to various Chicago area cultural arts organizations.

A longtime resident of Winnetka, Illinois, Mr. Piper has completed many years of service to that community as member and chairman of the Design Review Board, member and chairman of the Plan Commission, and as a village trustee.